Mammals
of Great Smoky Mountains
National Park

Mamm

THE UNIVERSITY OF TENNESSEE PRESS

This volume is published with the support of the
Great Smoky Mountains Conservation Association

als of Great Smoky
Mountains National Park

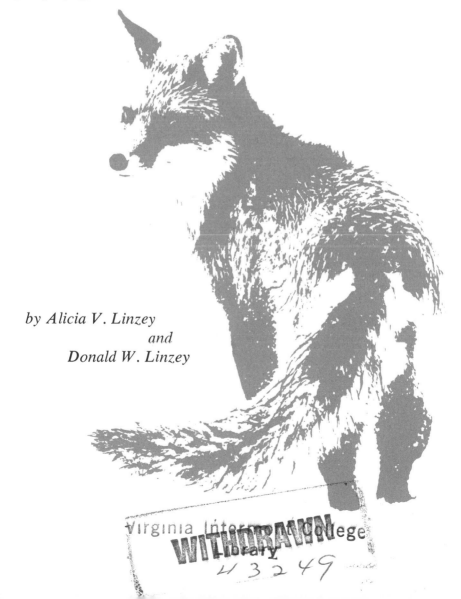

by Alicia V. Linzey
and
Donald W. Linzey

To Arthur Stupka

*In recognition of his immeasurable
contribution to the knowledge of the
natural history of the Great Smoky
Mountains National Park*

Preface

The first extensive mammal survey of the Great Smoky Mountains National Park was undertaken between 1931 and 1933 and resulted in the publication of a scientific paper on Smokies mammals (Komarek and Komarek, 1938). Since that time, there have been several published notes regarding particular species of Park mammals, and unpublished reports of numerous individuals have continued to swell Park files.

The authors have been the most recent mammalogists to work in the Park. Although our data were obtained from various localities throughout the Park, the greater percentage of time was spent in the eastern half. Our studies began in June 1963 and have extended to the present time. This research has resulted in several publications (see Literature Cited), among them a comprehensive paper including all available information on Great Smokies' mammals (Linzey and Linzey, 1968). The purpose of this book, then, is to make this information available to the Park visitor who wishes to become acquainted with the distribution and habits of the various types of Great Smokies' mammals. Technical information regarding parasites, measurements, and the like has not generally been included, and the reader is referred to our scientific publication for this information.

This account is not intended to serve as a means of identifying mammal species, although information of that sort is occasionally given. Several excellent field guides for that purpose are readily available. Scientific names used in the text are based on the *List of North American Recent Mammals* by Miller and Kellogg (1955), unless a more recent taxonomic revision has occurred. *The Mammal Guide* (Palmer, 1954) was used as a basis for common names.

Mammals of Great Smoky Mountains National Park is one of a series of books summarizing information pertaining to the natural history of the Park. Books previously published in this series include *Notes on the Birds of Great Smoky Mountains National Park* (Stupka, 1963), *Trees, Shrubs, and Woody Vines of Great Smoky Mountains National Park* (Stupka, 1964), and *Amphibians and*

Reptiles of Great Smoky Mountains National Park (Huheey and Stupka, 1967), all published by the University of Tennessee Press.

The authors are deeply indebted to Arthur Stupka, former Park Biologist, for his many suggestions during the course of our research and for his aid in preparing the manuscript. If it were not for his keen interest in the fauna of the Great Smokies, much of the information reported here would never have been recorded. We also wish to thank Mr. George Iannarone, Curator of Mammals, Chicago Academy of Sciences, and Dr. Charles O. Handley, Jr., Curator of Mammals, United States National Museum, for making available specimens and data from their respective collections. Finally, we are grateful to the National Park Service for the opportunity to carry on our study of mammals of the Park and to the numerous Park employees who have contributed information and specimens over the years.

Contents

ILLUSTRATIONS

Introduction

ECOLOGICAL HISTORY

The Great Smoky Mountains National Park is an area richly endowed with varied and abundant plant and animal life. The protection afforded by the Park has allowed a few mammal species to increase to considerable numbers, while others have declined as a result of the decrease of human influence. It is both interesting and worthwhile to study the alterations that have occurred in the ecology of the Park since the area was first settled and, in general, to relate this history to the changes in mammal life.

Prior to the mid-1700's, the area now composing the Park was largely uninhabited, although the Cherokee Indians lived nearby in such communities as Cherokee and along the Little Tennessee River. The Cherokees probably hunted to some extent, but they undoubtedly had little effect on the overall mammal populations. The ecology of the area began to be altered more extensively when settlers started arriving in greater numbers during the mid- to late 1700's. Their activities in clearing land for homesteads and cultivation greatly increased the diversity of mammal habitats, especially at lower elevations. This marked the beginning of a trend that was not to be reversed until acquisition of land for the Park commenced in the 1920's. Human habitation of the area increased throughout the nineteenth century, and the changes thereby wrought accelerated steadily. This trend reached a peak in the early 1900's, when the activities of logging companies drastically altered large tracts of land in a very short time. By the time the Park was dedicated in 1940, it has been estimated that more than two-thirds of the land had been cut over. The remaining "primeval" areas were largely confined to the highest elevations, including two large areas—one around Mt. Guyot and the other immediately southwest of Cades Cove.

The settlement of the mountains, with its accompanying influence on the land, undoubtedly had a substantial effect on mammal populations. Although there is little documented evidence of these effects, our present knowledge of the ecology of the various species indicates

Great Smoky Mountains National Park

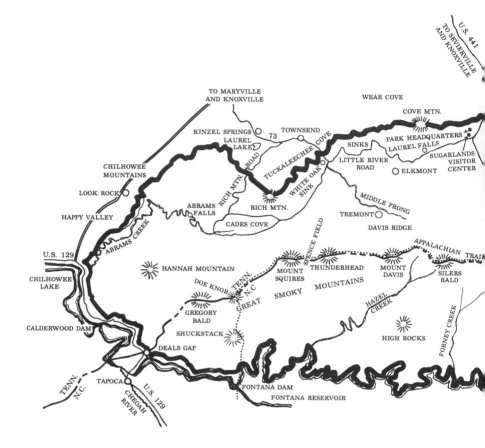

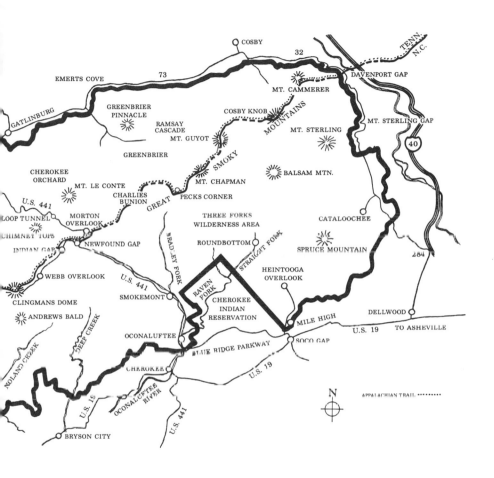

Map reproduced from Carlos C. Campbell,
Birth of a National Park
(The University of Tennessee Press, Knoxville, 2d printing, 1970)

the changes that must have occurred. Settlement of the Park area had a direct effect on some animals; for example, the gray wolf, river otter, and mountain lion were victims of hunting and trapping. On the other hand, populations of several game or fur species, such as the black bear, opossum, squirrels, raccoon, and foxes, apparently withstood these pressures. The mammals in the Park region were also affected in a more indirect fashion. As land at lower elevations was cleared and cut over, a different type of mammal habitat was created. Species that inhabit open areas or forest edges were able to extend their ranges into these new areas. The white-tailed deer, characteristically an animal of the forest edge, was one species that benefited from land-clearing operations. Deer were undoubtedly rare in the Great Smokies when the area was densely forested, but they apparently became fairly abundant during the 1800's. Land cleared for cultivation and subsequently abandoned was also particularly hospitable for certain species of small mammals, such as the little short-tailed shrew, eastern harvest mouse, rice rat, and common cotton rat.

Further, the decline of the American chestnut was another factor that seriously affected a number of mammal species. The chestnut blight fungus apparently arrived in the area in the mid-1920's (Woods and Shanks, 1957), and it has been estimated that by 1938, 85% of the chestnut trees in the Park had been killed or affected by the blight (F. H. Miller, 1938). Mammal species such as squirrels and bears that had depended upon chestnut mast for their food supply were gradually forced to depend on acorns instead. In some years, however, oak trees fail to bear fruit; when this occurs, animals are forced to leave the confines of the Park in search of food and hence become subjected to a higher mortality rate. Fortunately, such a mast failure is not a frequent occurrence.

When the Komarek brothers began working in the Great Smokies in 1931, the area was already in the process of reversion that has continued to the present time. As private lands were purchased for addition to the Park, homesteads were abandoned and logging operations ceased. As the processes of ecological succession took place, cleared lands gradually reverted to a forested condition. At present, it is considered that almost all of the Great Smokies' vegetation is in the climax stage (Whittaker, 1956). This means that the plant communities presently occurring in the Park will remain relatively stable as long as climatic and topographic conditions do not change significantly. The only major exception to this situation has been in Cades Cove, where fields are intentionally kept open by grazing and cultivation.

Much of the Komareks' work was concentrated in the Greenbrier section of the Park, a large portion of which had been under cultivation. Their trapping efforts revealed the presence of several small mammal species that rarely, if ever, have been collected again. Recently, E. V. Komarek returned to Greenbrier and retrapped some of their former study areas (personal communication, December 15, 1964). He related that much of Greenbrier showed a lack of specimens altogether, the exclusion of agriculture and fire having changed habitats considerably. Fields that once supported a dense growth of broomsedge are now covered by uniform stands of even-aged, young yellow-poplar trees.

Other mammal species have largely benefited from the effects of protection and reforestation. Due to hunting and other factors, the white-tailed deer population in the area had declined almost to the point of extirpation just prior to the establishment of the Park. Since coming under Park protection, however, deer have been increasing and populations are now well established in the Cades Cove area. They are still rather scarce in forested areas of the Park where habitats are not as suitable. Growth of oak forests in areas where the American chestnut has disappeared undoubtedly had a beneficial effect on mast-eating animals, such as squirrels and bears. Many forest-dwelling species of small mammals have also profited by the extension of their habitats.

The present distribution of mammal species in the Park area is directly related to the types of habitats available, and the occurrence and extent of each habitat depend upon various climatic and historical factors. Local climatic conditions vary widely in an area that ranges from 857 ft. to 6643 ft. above sea level. Since mean temperatures decrease with elevation at an average rate of 2.23°F per 1000 feet, sea-level climates most nearly equivalent to those of high elevations in the Smokies may occur about 1000 miles to the northeast, in northeastern Maine (Shanks, 1954). Annual precipitation also varies greatly, ranging from about 55 inches (Gatlinburg) to about 85 inches (Clingmans Dome). It is this variability that creates conditions favorable to the existence of such a great variety of plant and animal life in the Smokies and helps to explain why the ranges of a number of northern species extend down the Appalachian Mountain chain and reach or approach their southern limit in the Park area. Of course, the Great Smokies also play host to southern species of mammals as well as to those of wide geographic distribution. The presence of such a variety of mammal species in the Park, however, cannot be explained merely by present climatic conditions. During the Pleistocene epoch, which began approximately one million years ago, northern areas were periodically covered by extensive ice sheets. During the periods of advancing glaciation, the ranges of many species of plants and animals were slowly displaced southward. Since the glacial advances halted far north of the Smokies, the Southern Appalachians became a refuge for species that had previously been typical of more northern areas. With the retreat of the glaciers, the ranges of many of these forms then expanded northward where climates were again hospitable. Since climatic conditions at high elevations in the southern mountains are similar to those in northern areas, populations of northern species have persisted in the Great Smokies to the present day.

PREVIOUS MAMMAL STUDIES

The first extensive mammal survey of the Park area was undertaken by E. V. and R. Komarek, under the auspices of the Chicago Academy of Sciences and the University of Chicago. Preliminary field work carried out between March 30 and April 25, 1931, was largely limited to the Greenbrier and Smokemont areas. In February 1932 a headquarters was established at Greenbrier and the study continued in various parts of the Park for the next two years. This survey resulted in the publication of *Mammals of the Great Smoky Mountains* (Komarek and Komarek, 1938). Later work by Raymond J. Fleetwood, who was a wildlife technician associated with the Civilian Conservation Corps, covered the period from May 1934 to June 1935. He recorded species of birds and mammals observed during extensive hiking trips, and the daily journal that he kept is in the Park files. As part of a natural history study of Tennessee mammals, W. M. Perrygo and C. Lingebach of the United States National Museum worked in the Park from June 18 to July 5, 1937. The majority of the 112 specimens collected were taken in the eastern section. These data are included in *Annotated List of Tennessee Mammals* (Kellogg, 1939).

A major source of information about Park mammals has been the personal nature journal of Arthur Stupka, former chief naturalist and park biologist for the Great Smoky Mountains National Park. This journal was kept for twenty-eight years (1935–1963) and included not only personal observations but also substantiated reports of others. Copies of the journal reside in the Park files and in the library of the United States Department of the Interior.

Mammals

of Great Smoky Mountains
National Park

Opossums
FAMILY DIDELPHIDAE

Only one member of this marsupial family is found in the United States and, thus, in the Great Smoky Mountains National Park. The 'possum is probably best known for its habit of feigning death when injured or in a dangerous position. This can cause an enemy to turn its attention elsewhere long enough for the Opossum to scramble to a place of safety.

Since these animals are marsupials, they have a number of characteristics in common with other marsupials such as kangaroos, koala bears, and wombats, all of which are found in Australia. Female marsupials have a pouch or marsupium on their abdomen in which they carry their young. Furthermore, marsupials have an extremely short gestation period and the young are born in a very small and immature condition. Marsupials also exhibit a number of internal modifications that serve to differentiate them from other mammals.

Opossums are excellent climbers and are active mainly after dark. These animals are omnivorous and have an extremely varied diet that includes carrion, insects, amphibians, reptiles, fruit, berries, and many other items.

OPOSSUM
Didelphis marsupialis

The only representative of its family in the Great Smoky Mountains National Park, the Opossum has been called our "most abundant furbearer" (Komarek and Komarek, 1938). Although outwardly slow and stupid, this tenacious animal has extended its range northward in the past few decades, being hindered only by cold weather. Many individuals lose parts of their ears and tails as a result of exposure to freezing temperatures. The Opossum has a very muscular prehensile tail and an opposable "big toe" on each hind foot.

This species ranges throughout most of the Park, but the Komareks found it in diminishing numbers at higher elevations. It prefers to live near old fields and in open woods along streams. Opossums have been observed in the Park at elevations ranging from 1550 ft. to 6200 ft. Representative localities include The Sinks (1550 ft.), Cades Cove (1750 ft.), Tremont, Greenbrier (2000 ft.), Smokemont, Elkmont (2500 ft.), and Clingmans Dome Road (6200 ft.).

By examining feces, Komarek and Komarek (1938) established that a large part of the diet of Opossums in late summer and fall consists of blackberries (*Rubus allegheniensis*), pokeberries (*Phytolacca decandra*), wild grapes (*Vitis* sp.), and persimmons (*Diospyros virginiana*). These authors also concluded that the carrion-eating habit of Opossums was quite pronounced because the traps became increasingly effective after the bait decomposed. Stupka has noted several additional food items. The stomach of a specimen found dead along Little River near Tremont Junction contained a fair-sized water snake (*Natrix sipedon*). One of two individuals discovered near Park Headquarters had eaten a screech owl (*Otus asio*), while the second specimen contained a worm snake (*Carphophis amoenus*), an American toad (*Bufo americanus*), and a millipede. Stupka also observed an Opossum near Sugarlands eating wood frogs (*Rana sylvatica*), which had been killed on the wet road.

The gestation period of the Opossum is only 12 or 13 days, and the young are born in a very immature condition. Palmer (1954) states that new-born individuals are so small that 20 can easily fit into a teaspoon. Immediately after birth, they climb into the mother's pouch, where they remain for the next two to three months. After leaving the pouch, the young Opossums very often climb upon the mother's back where they cling to her fur as she carries them about. The Komareks noted a female with 13 naked young in her pouch on March 18 and a female that contained 8 embryos on February 23. Stupka recorded three observations of young Opossums. On February 4, 1936, he saw a half-grown specimen at Fighting Creek Gap, and on September 11, 1936, near Townsend, Tennessee, he observed a litter of Opossums about the size of half-grown house rats. On May 27, 1937, a female found dead near Park Headquarters had two young in her pouch, the larger of which measured just less than 1 inch in length.

Illustration Number 1

Shrews

FAMILY SORICIDAE

Eight species of shrews occur within the Great Smoky Mountains National Park. Ranging in size from the Pigmy Shrew (*Microsorex hoyi*), whose weight is approximately 1/12 ounce, to the Big Short-tailed Shrew (*Blarina brevicauda*) weighing ½ to ¾ ounce, these are the dwarfs of the mammal world.

A shrew is most readily recognized by its long tapering snout, tiny eyes, ears that are barely visible, and teeth having exposed tips stained a dark chestnut color. Unlike a mole, which it resembles to some extent, a shrew has feet that are all the same size.

Shrews may be active at any time of the day or night and at all seasons of the year. Some, like the Big Short-tailed Shrew, appear to be present in practically all habitats.

All shrews have scent glands on the sides of their body. These glands are responsible for a musky odor that is believed to be a means of communication between individuals, especially during the breeding season. This odor is most noticeable in the Big Short-tailed Shrew.

Shrews are largely carnivorous, feeding upon insects, earthworms, and other invertebrates. In turn, they are fed upon by owls, hawks, snakes, weasels, skunks, opossums, bobcats, and foxes.

COMMON SHREW
Sorex cinereus

The Common Shrew is best recognized by its small size (it weighs less than 1/5 ounce) and relatively long tail. Essentially a northern species, this animal ranges through the Appalachians as far south as Highlands, North Carolina.

The Common Shrew is generally distributed in wooded habitats at the upper elevations, being found in both deciduous and evergreen forests. Although the majority of specimens have been taken above 3000 ft. elevation, several individuals have been taken at Smoke-

mont (2200 ft.). Komarek and Komarek (1938) reported speci-
mens from many of the highest peaks, including Clingmans Dome,
Mt. Kephart, Mt. Guyot, and Mt. Collins. Other areas where the
Common Shrew has been taken include Greenbrier, Dry Sluice Gap,
Buck Fork (4500 ft.), Flat Creek (4900 ft.), Walker Prong, Indian
Gap (5200 ft.), between Forney Ridge and Andrews Bald (6000
ft.), and Old Black Mountain (6300 ft.). On December 7, 1935,
Stupka found two of these shrews in Gatlinburg (1300 ft.), outside
the Park boundary.

SMOKY SHREW
Sorex fumeus

Although the Smoky Shrew inhabits practically all altitudes, it ap-
pears to be most plentiful at the middle and high elevations in the
Park. Streamsides and fairly moist situations, both in evergreen and
deciduous forests, are a favored habitat. Like the Common Shrew
(*Sorex cinereus*), this species is near the southern limit of its range
in the Great Smoky Mountains National Park. The only records
south of the Park are from Brasstown Bald (4700 ft.), Georgia
(Jackson, 1928), and near Highlands, North Carolina (Odum,
1949). This boreal species has been recorded from elevations as
low as 1000 ft. in the southeast at High Cliff, Campbell County,
Tennessee (Howell, 1909), and Jocassee, Oconee County, South
Carolina (Schwartz, 1955).

During the summer, the Smoky Shrew is dull brown above and
paler below, while in winter the pelage is a uniform gray. The bicolor tail is yellowish below and brown above. Komarek and
Komarek (1938) noted specimens in winter pelage during February, March, April, and October.

The breeding season of the Smoky Shrew extends from early
spring to fall. As many as eight young, each weighing approximately
1/200 ounce, may constitute a litter. Komarek and Komarek (1938)
recorded a large nursing female on October 12 at an altitude of
6200 ft. In 1963, the authors discovered nursing females near the
Cosby Campground (2000 ft.) on July 1 and at Low Gap (4242
ft.) on July 17.

Illustration Number 2

SOUTHEASTERN SHREW
Sorex longirostris

The Southeastern Shrew is among the rarest shrews in the Great Smoky Mountains National Park. Only three specimens have been recorded. On June 5, 1934, R. J. Fleetwood discovered one in Greenbrier. This specimen, a male, was found dead in a post hole located in a sedge field at an elevation of about 1600 ft. A second individual was picked up in the same area by Dr. M. S. Crowder on February 4, 1938. The most recent specimen was obtained by D. W. Pfitzer near Park Headquarters on September 19, 1950. This shrew may not be so rare in this area as Park records indicate, since Tuttle (1964a) captured 26 Southeastern Shrews 10 miles southwest of Knoxville, Knox County, Tennessee.

The Southeastern Shrew is dark brown with paler underparts. It closely resembles the Common Shrew, *Sorex cinereus*, being slightly smaller and more reddish in color. This similarity may easily result in misidentification. Kellogg (1939), after studying a series of these shrews, concluded that the supposed distinctions were due to individual variation. However, Hall and Kelson (1959) regard *Sorex longirostris* as a distinct species.

LONG-TAILED SHREW
Sorex dispar

The Long-tailed Shrew, dark grayish with slightly paler underparts and with a nearly uniform colored tail, was first recorded in the Great Smoky Mountains National Park in October 1932 when R. V. Komarek found a specimen on Clingmans Dome. He identified it as the Smoky Shrew (*Sorex fumeus*)—a species with which it can easily be confused. Eighteen years passed before Conaway and Pfitzer, while making a careful examination of the shrews in the Park's collection, recognized the true identity of this specimen. A few months later these men found a number of Long-tailed Shrews along the West Prong of the Little Pigeon River, close to the trans-mountain road (Tennessee side), at elevations above 3700 ft. Others were discovered at approximately 4400 ft. on the North Carolina side of that same highway and between 6400 and 6642 ft. on Clingmans Dome (Conaway and Pfitzer, 1952). In March 1962 three additional specimens were taken by M. D. Tuttle at Greenbrier.

Apparently these little mammals are not rare in the cool, damp, rocky habitat that prevails in those localities.

The discovery of these shrews in the Park represented a range extension of almost 200 miles southward in the Appalachian Mountains. This species had not previously been recorded south of Raleigh County, West Virginia, where it was collected by A. H. Howell in 1909 (Kellogg, 1937). Schwartz (1956) subsequently recorded two additional specimens from near Wagon Road Gap, Haywood County, North Carolina, at an elevation of 4525 ft. An additional record of this shrew in Tennessee was contributed by Conaway and Howell (1953), who collected one specimen at Roan Mountain, Carter County, at 4800 ft.

Like other members of the family, the Long-tailed Shrew is largely carnivorous. Conaway and Pfitzer (1952) reported finding beetles and spiders in the stomachs and intestines of six specimens taken in the Park.

NORTHERN WATER SHREW
Sorex palustris

The paucity of information concerning the Northern Water Shrew makes it difficult to determine its true status in the Park. From the few records, one would infer that it occurs in highly localized populations. However, a careful search may reveal a more widespread distribution than is known at present. The habitat of the more or less aquatic Northern Water Shrew is the margins of swiftly flowing mountain streams, where this blackish-gray animal dwells beneath the overhanging banks and in rock crevices. A characteristic that distinguishes this species from all other shrews in the Park is the fringe of hairs along the outer margins of the hind feet; the fringe presumably aids the animal in swimming.

In November and December 1950, Conaway and Pfitzer (1952) discovered a few of these shrews along the bank of the West Prong of the Little Pigeon River, less than a mile below the confluence with Alum Cave Creek. That proved to be not only a new Park record but also a new state (Tennessee) record. Furthermore, it represented a southward range extension of approximately 200 miles, since this species had not previously been recorded south of West Virginia (Hooper, 1942). Further investigation by Conaway and Pfitzer and by the authors has revealed this shrew living beneath overhanging banks and in rock crevices along the West Prong of the Little Pigeon River and its tributaries from 3700 ft. to 4700 ft. elevations.

PIGMY SHREW
Microsorex hoyi

The distinction of being the rarest shrew in the Great Smoky Mountains National Park belongs to the Pigmy Shrew. An adult weighs only approximately 1/12 ounce and reaches a total length of 3 to 3½ inches. It is the smallest mammal inhabiting North America. The Pigmy Shrew is grayish-brown or gray above and paler below and is quite often mistaken for the Common Shrew (*Sorex cinereus*).

Until recently, this shrew had never been reported from the Park. It had been collected a few miles southeast of the Park in Pisgah National Forest, North Carolina (Hamilton, 1943; Brimley, 1944). Smith, Funderburg, and Quay (1960) noted that it was uncommon in North Carolina, inhabiting moist forests. It was not until 1968 that a previously unreported specimen of the Pigmy Shrew from the Park was discovered in the collections of the University of Illinois Museum of Natural History (Hoffmeister, 1968). It had been taken on September 6, 1941, at Newfound Gap, Swain County, North Carolina.

BIG SHORT-TAILED SHREW
Blarina brevicauda

From the standpoint of weight, this is our largest shrew. (Because of its much longer tail, the Northern Water Shrew is somewhat longer.) The Big Short-tailed Shrew is a large stocky shrew with 32 chestnut-tipped teeth, very small external ears, and tiny eyes that are light-sensitive only (Palmer, 1954). Although it is rarely observed, this secretive animal is one of the most widely distributed mammals in the Park. Many of the tunnel openings one is likely to observe in the forest floor are made by this shrew.

The Big Short-tailed Shrew occupies almost all types of habitats at all elevations. Signs of this animal can be most frequently seen in moist areas with some leaf litter and low herbaceous vegetation. Odum (1949), in reviewing the status of this shrew in the Highlands, North Carolina, area, noted that it preferred moist habitats during the summer, being found especially along streams in mature forests. None were discovered in dry fields.

A little-known fact about the Big Short-tailed Shrew is that it is the only North American mammal equipped with poison glands. The poison, produced by the submaxillary glands, is present in the saliva; apparently it plays a part in the capturing of prey. Mice and rabbits injected with submaxillary gland secretion exhibited a local reaction, lowering of the blood pressure, slowing of the heart, and inhibition of respiration (Pearson, 1942). Few records are available concerning the effect of this poison on man, although the bite may cause considerable discomfort and has been known to produce local swelling (Maynard, 1889).

The musky odor common to all shrews is particularly pronounced in this species and consequently few animals will eat it. Some predators, particularly the fox and bobcat, kill many of these little animals, and over the years dozens have been picked up along Park trails, especially at higher altitudes. On September 14, 1944, Stupka and members of a party he was guiding along the Appalachian Trail found seven freshly killed shrews of this species in 1½ miles (Newfound Gap to Mt. Kephart).

Remains of this shrew have been found in the stomachs of a copperhead (*Agkistrodon contortrix*) (Savage, 1967), a black rat snake (*Elaphe obsoleta*), and a spotted skunk (*Spilogale putorius*). The pellet of a barred owl (*Strix varia*) contained the remains of this shrew. On April 8, 1944, a barred owl sighted along Little River, above Elkmont, was carrying one of these large shrews (Stupka).

Illustration Number 3

LITTLE SHORT-TAILED SHREW
Cryptotis parva

The smaller of the two short-tailed shrews, the Little Short-tailed Shrew, is the shortest mammal in the Park. It looks like a small edition of the Big Short-tailed Shrew except that it has a shorter, more slender tail and only 30 instead of 32 chestnut-tipped teeth. Its tiny beady eyes are probably light-sensitive only (Palmer, 1954). It weighs the equivalent of two dimes (approximately 1/6 ounce).

This shrew is known to occur at elevations ranging from 1442 to

2730 ft. (Komarek and Komarek, 1938). The latter figure represents the highest elevation in the United States at which this shrew has been recorded (Hamilton, 1944). Localities it has been known to frequent include Cades Cove, Gatlinburg, Park Headquarters area (1500 ft.), Fighting Creek (1442 ft.), Elkmont, Greenbrier, and Fish Camp Prong (2730 ft.).

The status of the Little Short-tailed Shrew in the Park is a subject that needs further investigation. The specimens reported by Komarek and Komarek (1938) occurred in fallow field situations. Along Fighting Creek near Gatlinburg, these shrews were found at the bases of pines and small apple trees in moderately overgrown broomsedge fields. At Fish Camp Prong near Elkmont, they were located in an open grassy patch along the forest margin. If these habitats are representative of the areas preferred by the Little Short-tailed Shrew, this species may be decreasing as cultivated areas yield to the regrowth of the forest.

Although the Little Short-tailed Shrew generally breeds all year in the South, the only data concerning breeding habits in the Park are supplied by Komarek and Komarek (1938), who found a female that had just finished nursing on October 16 and recorded four males in breeding condition on October 20.

A specific instance of predation was noted by Stupka, who on January 9, 1940, recovered a Little Short-tailed Shrew from the stomach of a screech owl (*Otus asio*) that was found dead on the transmountain road near Park Headquarters. On the morning of December 12, 1957, he found a dead shrew of this species on the snow just outside the Park boundary. It appeared to have succumbed to the extremely low overnight temperature, which was recorded as being 10°F below zero at Park Headquarters.

Moles

FAMILY TALPIDAE

Three species of moles occur within the Great Smoky Mountains National Park. Adaptations linked to their subterranean habits render these among the most interesting of our small mammals.

A mole can be recognized by its extremely large forefeet; apparent absence of eyes and ears; stout, tubular body; and very soft, thick fur. The presence of these mammals can be detected by low ridges and mounds of earth on the ground surface.

Moles are active at any hour and in every season. The preferred habitat varies with the species.

These animals feed upon earthworms, insects, and other small invertebrates. However, they are not exclusively carnivorous, since vegetable food will be eaten. Their fossorial habits probably protect them from extensive predation, although they may occasionally be eaten by birds, reptiles, or other mammals.

HAIRY-TAILED MOLE
Parascalops breweri

The Hairy-tailed Mole is best recognized by the character that gives it its common name—a short, hairy tail. It has a conical snout that is naked at the end. The eyes are not apparent and there are no external ears. This species is near the southern limit of its range in the Great Smoky Mountains National Park. A highly localized population has been reported at Highlands, North Carolina, approximately 40 miles south of the Park (Gordon and Bailey, 1963; Johnston, 1967). No specimens have been recorded from Georgia (Golley, 1962).

The first specimens recorded from the Park and from the state of Tennessee were found by Komarek and Komarek (1938). These moles were taken along Chapman Prong (3200 ft.) and Buck Fork under damp, mossy rocks in rhododendron thickets. The Komareks also observed tunnels made by this mole in soft soil covered with hemlock needles on Mt. Kephart (5200 ft.). Although Palmer (1954) stated that this species is found only to about 3000 ft. elevation in the Appalachians, records show that it ranges from 1565 to 6250 ft. in the Park. Representative locality records include The Sinks (1565 ft.), Cades Cove (1750 ft.), Sugarlands (2000 ft.), Elkmont (2200 ft., 2500 ft.), Rainbow Falls Trail (3000 ft.), Alum Cave Trail (4300 ft.), Spence Field (5000 ft.), Newfound Gap (5050 ft.), Blanket Mountain, Mt. Kephart (5200 ft.), Mt. Collins (5500 ft.), and Mt. Buckley (6250 ft.).

Only one specific instance of predation upon this mole has been recorded here. An individual found dead on the road between New-found Gap and Indian Gap on September 24, 1950, had not been run over by a car but had apparently been killed by a fox, since fox scats were found beside the animal (Pfitzer, 1950).

EASTERN MOLE
Scalopus aquaticus

The Eastern Mole is similar in appearance to the Hairy-tailed Mole (*Parascalops breweri*), the major distinction being that its short tail is nearly devoid of hair. Two other differences are that the nostrils open upward and the eyes are completely covered with skin. Although recorded from only five areas in the Park, this species seems to be common at certain of these localities.

Tunnels made by this mole were examined by the Komareks in fields below 1500 ft. (outside the Park), where the soil was somewhat sandy. Specific localities outside the Park include Dry Valley, Blount County, Tennessee (1200 ft.), and Gatlinburg, Sevier County, Tennessee (1300 ft., 1400 ft., and 1600 ft.). Paul and Quay (1963) found this species at 3000 ft. in the Toxaway River Gorge, North Carolina, which is southeast of the Park. Howell (1909), however, noted that runways were frequently seen as high as 4500 ft. on Brasstown Bald, Georgia.

The Eastern Mole has been found in the Park between 1750 and 2700 ft. The first specimen was taken at Greenbrier in 1936. Other localities include Cades Cove (1750 ft.), Metcalf Bottoms (2000 ft.), and near Cosby (2700 ft.). This mole is apparently quite common in the field adjoining the Oconaluftee Pioneer Museum (2100 ft.), where during the summers of 1950 and 1960, 10 and 20 of these animals, respectively, were recorded.

Illustration Number 4

STAR-NOSED MOLE
Condylura cristata

This animal, the rarest of the three moles that inhabit the Great Smoky Mountains National Park, can easily be recognized by the 22 fleshy, sensory processes on its snout. No other mammal possesses these unique structures. The fur is glossy black or dark brown, the eyes are small but apparent, and the ears are barely evident externally. The tail is well haired and constricted near the body. This species was not listed by Komarek and Komarek (1938). In commenting on the mammals of Highlands, North Carolina, Odum (1949) stated that this mole is probably fairly common, although he examined only one specimen.

The preferred habitat of the Star-nosed Mole includes moist woodlands, damp meadows, swamps, and bogs. The first individual found in the Park was taken along Deep Creek (2200 ft.) in October 1934 (Fleetwood). This mammal has since been reported from localities ranging in elevation from 1600 to 5500 ft. In September 1950 a specimen was taken along the Little River Road (1600 ft.). On two occasions, in 1961 and 1964, a dead Star-nosed Mole was found along the Appalachian Trail near Charlies Bunion (5500 ft.). Other localities include Smokemont, Kephart Prong Hatchery (2800 ft.), and the Appalachian Trail between Newfound Gap and Indian Gap (5300 ft.).

Two specific cases of predation on this mole have been recorded in the Park. In September 1950 Stupka removed a Star-nosed Mole from a corn snake (*Elaphe guttata*) found dead along the Little River Road near Metcalf Bottoms. Stupka also noted one of these moles that had been killed by a cat at Smokemont in June 1943.

Bats

FAMILY VESPERTILIONIDAE

Eight species of bats have been recorded in the Park, all belonging to the same family. These animals, along with birds and insects, have evolved the power of true flight. The wing of a bat, unlike that of a bird, is supported by the hind limbs and body, as well as by the forelimbs and digits.

The capacity for flight renders these mammals extremely mobile, a fact that is reflected in the enormous ranges of many species. Like birds, some bats migrate long distances to seek more favorable conditions during the winter months. Other species may remain in their summer range but pass the cold season in hibernation, a state characterized by a deathlike sleep during which the metabolism is greatly reduced. All species found in the Park are believed to hibernate except the migratory Red and Silver-haired Bats (*Lasiurus borealis* and *Lasionycteris noctivagans*, respectively). Bats have been seen in flight over the Park during every month of the year.

The reproductive process in bats is unusual and interesting. Several species are known to mate during the late summer and fall, the sperm being stored throughout the winter. Ovulation, however, does not occur until spring, and fertilization supposedly takes place at this time also (Wimsatt, 1942; 1944). A second mating may occur in the spring.

The Vespertilionid bats seem to be exclusively insectivorous. They generally rest during the day and emerge at dusk to fly about erratically in search of insects. Presumably, their ability to use "radar" aids them in detecting obstacles in their path, which may in some cases be food items.

Bats appear to have few predators. Hamilton (1943) noted that Big Brown Bats (*Eptesicus fuscus*) are sometimes eaten by barn owls (*Tyto alba*) and discussed an instance where a black rat snake (*Elaphe obsoleta*) decimated a colony of these bats.

The discovery that bats are major carriers of rabies has stimulated much interest in the biology of these forms. At present, comparatively little is known of their habits.

LITTLE BROWN MYOTIS
Myotis lucifugus

The three bats in the Park belonging to the genus *Myotis* are quite difficult to distinguish from one another. The ears of the Little Brown Myotis are moderate in size and when laid forward, they reach to the nostril. The hairs on the back of this bat characteristically have glossy tips.

The Little Brown Myotis can also be identified while flying by its seemingly feeble and erratic flight pattern. It has been recorded from only five localities in the Park. Cades Cove (1750 ft.), Saltpeter Cave (1750 ft.), and Elkmont have yielded single specimens. Two individuals were taken by the Komareks at Greenbrier. On two consecutive days in December, C. E. Mohr counted 10 and 20 of these bats in Blowhole Cave, Whiteoak Sink. Odum (1949) noted that the Little Brown Myotis is probably fairly common in the Highlands, North Carolina, area, although only one individual had been collected.

KEEN'S MYOTIS
Myotis keenii

This species, which nears the southern limit of its range in this area, has been taken in the Park on only two occasions. However, according to Hamilton (1943), this species may be more abundant over its range than the number of specimens in collections would indicate. Keen's Myotis is a dark brown bat and can be distinguished from the other two *Myotis* in the Park by the size of its ears. When laid forward, the ears extend approximately 1/16 of an inch beyond the nose. In contrast to the Little Brown Myotis, this species has a strong and direct flight.

Both Park specimens were taken in Tennessee. The first individual was found dead near Park Headquarters on March 10, 1938. The second was taken on December 3, 1950, at Blowhole Cave in Whiteoak Sink.

Although Keen's Myotis has not been taken on the North Carolina side of the Park, two specimens have been reported from nearby areas. Miller and Allen (1928) recorded an individual from Cherokee, Swain County, North Carolina, which is adjacent to the Park boundary. Schwartz (1954) recorded this bat from Talc Mountain, 14 miles northeast of Andrews, Swain County, North Carolina.

INDIANA BAT
Myotis sodalis

The Indiana Bat, which closely resembles the Little Brown Myotis, has been found in great numbers in the Great Smoky Mountains National Park. Its habit of congregating in caves in large numbers gives this species another of its common names, the Social Bat.

The Indiana Bat was first collected in the Park at Park Headquarters on September 2, 1937. On December 2, 1950, C. E. Mohr and others exploring Blowhole Cave in Whiteoak Sink estimated that there were 500 of these bats present. Upon returning the following day, they counted 2,242 individuals in this cave.

SILVER-HAIRED BAT
Lasionycteris noctivagans

The Silver-haired Bat is best recognized by its pelage, which is dark brown with silver-tipped hairs. Its flight pattern has a distinctive fluttery quality, with frequent darts, twists, and glides (Palmer, 1954). Hamilton (1943) stated that this species probably does not commonly occur south of the Smoky Mountains during summer, but possibly winters in the Gulf states.

This migratory bat has been reported in the Park only nine times. The first three individuals were taken by the Komareks in Cades Cove (2000 ft.) and Greenbrier. Other localities that have yielded specimens are Whitcoak Sink, Park Headquarters, Deep Creek Ranger Station (1900 ft.), and Meigs Creek (2500 ft.). In 1962 the first and only high-altitude record resulted from the discovery of a dead Silver-haired Bat on the Appalachian Trail between Newfound Gap and Indian Gap.

Palmer (1954) stated that this bat probably does not breed in the southern two-thirds of the United States, except perhaps in the mountains. No young have been reported from the Park.

EASTERN PIPISTRELLE
Pipistrellus subflavus

The Eastern Pipistrelle, the smallest of our bats, is fairly common in the Great Smoky Mountains National Park. Kellogg (1939) stated that it is "one of the most widely distributed bats in the State [Tennessee]." This species can easily be identified by the distinctive tricolor pattern of the fur. The individual hairs are dark at the base and tip with a wide lighter zone in between. The flight of these bats is weak and erratic (Palmer, 1954).

Specimens have been collected in several caves near Cades Cove, as well as in the Cosby (1750 ft.), Greenbrier, and Sugarlands areas. On two consecutive days in December, C. E. Mohr counted 103 and 145 of these bats in Blowhole Cave, Whiteoak Sink. Kellogg (1939) captured two individuals near Low Gap (2700 ft.), the highest elevation at which the Eastern Pipistrelle has been recorded in the Park.

BIG BROWN BAT
Eptesicus fuscus

The Big Brown Bat has been reported infrequently in the Great Smoky Mountains National Park, although Odum (1949) stated that this species is common in the Highlands, North Carolina, area. A medium-sized bat with dark brown fur, the Big Brown Bat has a wingspread of approximately 12 inches. The size and color of this bat distinguish it from all others in the Park. The flight is strong and is marked by frequent and sudden changes in direction (Palmer, 1954).

Only seven specimens of this bat have been recorded in the Park. The first individual was taken by the Komareks at Greenbrier on November 1, 1932. This species has also been found at Park Headquarters, Cosby (1750 ft.), Greenbrier (1900 ft., 2000 ft.), and Le Conte Lodge (6300 ft.).

The young of the Big Brown Bat are born during May in the South (Palmer, 1954). On August 9, 1964, the authors collected a male in breeding condition at the Cosby Ranger Station (1750 ft.).

RED BAT
Lasiurus borealis

One of the most beautiful of our bats, the Red Bat has been observed here on many occasions. The rusty red color of the fur gives this species its common name. In the Park, it has been found at elevations ranging from 1400 ft. to 4800 ft.

On July 29, 1963, the authors found an immature female in the Cosby area (1600 ft.). In September 1943 Stupka observed an individual sleeping in an oak sapling on Thomas Ridge (4800 ft.). These bats have also been reported from Twentymile Creek, Sugarlands (1600 ft.), Cades Cove (1750 ft.), Greenbrier (1800 ft.), and Kephart Prong. Ganier and Clebsch (1946) recorded two Red Bats at Stratton Meadow Gap (4350 ft.) in the Unicoi Mountains, just south of the western limits of the Great Smoky Mountains National Park.

Palmer (1954) noted that the Red Bat is a nonhibernating migratory tree bat that migrates northward in April and May and southward in October and November. However, there have been a number of winter sight records in the Park. These bats have also been observed in flight and feeding during the daylight hours.

Illustration Number 5

EASTERN LUMP-NOSED BAT
Corynorhinus rafinesquii

One of the most common bats occurring in the Park is the Eastern Lump-nosed Bat, named for the prominent bumps on top of its nose. This species can also be recognized by its very large ears and is often referred to as the Big-eared Bat.

Park records indicate that these animals inhabit areas ranging in elevation from 1750 to 2400 ft. They spend the daylight hours in caves, hollow trees, and buildings. A deserted house (1900 ft.) near Park Headquarters has yielded many individuals, as have caves in the Cades Cove area (1750 ft.). Other localities where these bats have been seen include Greenbrier and Forney Creek (2400 ft.). Although the latter locality represents the highest elevation at which this bat has been recorded in the Park, Odum (1949) recorded one specimen taken at Highlands, North Carolina, in August 1948 at 3850 ft.

The single young of the Eastern Lump-nosed Bat is born in May or June and remains with the female for approximately two months. On July 8, 1950, near Park Headquarters, J. C. Howell observed three female bats, each with a single young that was almost half as large as the parent. In the same area on July 16, 1950, Stupka saw a female carrying a juvenile that was more than half its size. The young individual was darker than the parent.

Illustration Number 6

Rabbits and Hares

FAMILY LEPORIDAE

The familiar long ears and large hind legs serve to distinguish this family. Two members of this group occur in the Great Smoky Mountains National Park—the Eastern Cottontail (*Sylvilagus floridanus*) and the New England Cottontail (*Sylvilagus transitionalis*). Though very similar in appearance, the New England Cottontail is smaller and has a dark patch between the ears.

A third species, the Varying Hare (*Lepus americanus*), was reported as occurring in the Park in former times, but no specimens have ever been taken. In 1888 Dr. C. H. Merriam reported that this species was unknown from the Smokies. However, Kellogg (1939) included this species in the Park on the basis of information received from local residents. They reported that hares were formerly present in the mountainous district extending from Mt. Guyot to White Rock (Mt. Cammerer), Cocke County, Tennessee. These hares were said to turn white in winter and to make long jumps when chased in the snow by dogs. They were usually "jumped" from rhododendron thickets near the summits of the peaks. Kellogg's record is listed by Hall and Kelson (1959) as being a marginal record for the species. Blair et al. (1968) also give the range as extending "south in Appalachian chain to eastern Tennessee." Smith, Funderburg, and Quay (1960) state that this species probably occurs in open brushy areas in mixed forests in the mountains of Virginia and Tennessee. Stupka is convinced that this hare is not here now, and he doubts that it was here in pre-Park days.

These mammals are primarily nocturnal and are active throughout the year. Although the hares are forest species, cottontail rabbits may be found in a variety of habitats. The members of this family are strict vegetarians and are preyed upon by many of the larger mammals, birds, and snakes; in unprotected areas they are hunted by man.

EASTERN COTTONTAIL
Sylvilagus floridanus

NEW ENGLAND COTTONTAIL
Sylvilagus transitionalis

Although two species of cottontail rabbits occur in the Park, these forms are so similar that a distinction is rarely made between them, the majority of Park records referring simply to "cottontail." For this reason, all information, excepting data specifically attributed to a particular species, is combined in this discussion. The knowledgeable observer can distinguish the New England Cottontail by its smaller size and its patch of dark fur between the ears.

Cottontails (*Sylvilagus* sp.) occur throughout the Park at all altitudes. Examples of localities where these rabbits are known to occur include Cosby (1750 ft.), Cades Cove (1750 ft.), Greenbrier (1900–2000 ft.), Noland Divide (5800 ft.), Collins Gap (6000 ft.), Clingmans Dome, and Mt. Le Conte (6593 ft.).

The New England Cottontail has been recorded from several localities in the vicinity of the Park. Howell (1909) collected one specimen at Brasstown Bald in northern Georgia at 4600 ft. Odum (1949) found this species at Highlands, North Carolina, but noted that its status was not well known. Paul and Quay (1963) recorded one individual from 1400 ft. in the Toxaway River Gorge.

Although the New England Cottontail had been taken in the mountains both north and south of the Park, it was not recorded by Komarek and Komarek (1938). They stated: "Local people asserted that two kinds of rabbits are found in the park and that one of these which inhabits the higher region is called the 'woods rabbit.' " The Komareks suggested that further investigation would probably establish its presence in this area. Kellogg (1939) recorded the first Park specimen—a New England Cottontail taken near Low Gap (3300 ft.). Since that time two additional specimens have been reported—one from Pine Knot Branch near Elkmont (2100 ft.) in September 1957, the other from the Alum Cave Parking Area in November 1960.

In discussing the Eastern Cottontail, the Komareks stated that it was most often found in open woods and broomsedge fields. Although Kellogg (1939) found one individual in a rhododendron thicket in hemlock woods, he noted that they were most abundant in abandoned farm fields overgrown with broomsedge, weeds, and brush; in brier patches; and in thickets bordering deciduous woods and small streams.

Young cottontails are born from late winter to early fall (Palmer, 1954). During the summer of 1938, a nest containing young was discovered on the summit of Mt. Le Conte. Young individuals have been observed in May and June, and half-grown cottontails have been noted in July and September.

Many of our larger snakes feed on these rabbits. On May 23, 1939, and June 13, 1940, Stupka observed black rat snakes (*Elaphe obsoleta*) feeding upon young cottontails. Half-grown rabbits were found in the stomachs of timber rattlesnakes (*Crotalus horridus*) in July 1942 and September 1947. Savage (1967) recorded Eastern Cottontails from three timber rattlesnakes. Komarek and Komarek (1938) reported fluctuating fox populations in the Greenbrier area possibly due to fluctuating cottontail populations.

Eastern Cottontail, *Illustration Number 7*

Marmots, Chipmunks, and Squirrels

FAMILY SCIURIDAE

All areas of the Park are inhabited by one or more of the seven members of this family occurring here. These members are variable in form and habits. Some are ground-dwelling, such as the Eastern Chipmunk (*Tamias striatus*) and Woodchuck (*Marmota monax*), while others, like the Gray Squirrel (*Sciurus carolinensis*) and the Red Squirrel (*Tamiasciurus hudsonicus*), nest in trees.

With the exception of the flying squirrels (*Glaucomys volans* and *Glaucomys sabrinus*), the activities of these animals are confined largely to the daytime. The seasonal activity pattern varies greatly throughout the year. Many species are abroad during all seasons, whereas others enter a winter sleep of varying depth. During the hot, dry months, some of the members of this family that dwell in the Far

West undergo a summer sleep, or aestivation, that corresponds to hibernation.

The members of this family may eat a wide variety of foods, although plants form the bulk of the diet of most species. The smaller forms are preyed upon by other mammals, as well as by snakes and birds. Man is the prime enemy of the larger species in unprotected areas.

WOODCHUCK
Marmota monax

The Woodchuck, or "groundhog," is a common resident of the Great Smoky Mountains National Park. It is a large stocky rodent with a flattened head and medium-length furred tail. The fur varies in color from yellowish to dark reddish brown, and the tips of the hairs are lighter, giving the animal a grizzled appearance. Locally, the Woodchuck is known as the "whistle-pig" because of the piercing whistle it occasionally emits before disappearing into its burrow. These burrows may also be used by cottontails, skunks, and foxes (Palmer, 1954).

Woodchucks have been seen from the lowest elevations to 6300 ft. Although they occur throughout the Park, they are most abundant in the open meadowlands and along the mowed roadsides at the lower elevations. Although less plentiful now than formerly, they may still be seen in the vicinity of almost all the former homesites. Woodchucks are occasionally found in dense forests, but are rare in the spruce-fir region. These rodents have been seen in the following representative localities: Park Headquarters (1500 ft.), Cades Cove (1750 ft.), Greenbrier, Deep Creek, Smokemont, Fighting Creek Gap (2500 ft.), Sugarlands (2500 ft.), Low Gap (2700 ft.), along the transmountain road (various elevations), Collins Gap (5700 ft.), Forney Ridge (6300 ft.), and Mt. Le Conte. These animals were quite numerous in 1934 in the vicinity of Black Camp Gap (4522 ft.), where Fleetwood observed up to 18 during a single hike.

Hamilton (1943) stated that the Woodchuck enters a long dormant period during the coldest months of the year. Active individuals have been seen in the Park throughout the year, but these animals are extremely scarce in very cold weather.

Breeding usually occurs in March and the young are born during

April and early May (Hamilton, 1943). Several records of young Woodchucks during the month of May indicate that they are approximately one-quarter to one-third grown at that time. Komarek and Komarek (1938), however, found a half-grown individual in August 1932.

Woodchucks feed upon grasses, clover, alfalfa, plantain, and various perennials (Hamilton, 1943). In 1932 the Komareks observed an individual eating clover. In 1934 Fleetwood watched these animals climb into small silverbell trees (*Halesia carolina*) and eat the bark.

Motor vehicles probably cause the greatest number of mortalities among Woodchucks in the Park. Along the boundaries of the Park, this animal is hunted for sport. In January 1938 Stupka found a Woodchuck that had recently been killed by a bobcat (*Lynx rufus*) above Big Cove (3200 ft.), an area just outside the Park boundary.

Illustration Number 8

EASTERN CHIPMUNK
Tamias striatus

The Eastern Chipmunk, our only ground squirrel, is frequently seen in the Park. It has a striped face and five dark and four light body stripes that end at the reddish rump. The rather sharp "chuck-chuck-chuck" call of the chipmunk is often heard along the trails. It is found at all elevations in the Park, but it is much less abundant in the spruce-fir forests than in the deciduous woodlands. It occupies such diverse habitats as rocky woodland, edges of grass balds and clearings, farm lands, and open woods.

Sight records for this mammal are numerous, including such localities as Cades Cove, Deep Creek, Smokemont, Elkmont (2500 ft.), Greenbrier (2500 ft.), Cosby (2700 ft.), Fort Harry Cliffs (3200 ft.), Sugarland Mountain (4400 ft.), Pin Oak Gap (4500 ft.), near Newfound Gap (5100 ft.), Mt. Guyot, and Clingmans Dome (6500 ft.). There is some indication that chipmunks, although common in many areas, are rare in certain localities. During an 18-year period, only one individual was seen on the summit of Mt. Le Conte. On September 25, 1950, chipmunks were seen in the Abrams Creek area for the first time in eight years.

The Eastern Chipmunk is active during the day and is, therefore, more frequently seen than our nocturnal mammals. These animals may sleep for long periods during the winter, but they do not hibernate. In the Park, chipmunks have been seen during every month of the year, but sight records are infrequent during December and early January.

Breeding in the Eastern Chipmunk occurs from "March onward," and the three to five young are born in a lined chamber in the burrow system (Palmer, 1954). On June 4, 1954, at Park Headquarters, Stupka saw an individual stuffing leaves into its cheek pouches, possibly to be used as nesting material.

Occasionally, entirely black (melanistic) or entirely white (albino) chipmunks are noted. In October 1934 Fleetwood reported that two melanistic individuals were seen near Townsend, Tennessee, just outside the Park; one of these had a white streak from the throat to the forefeet. An albino chipmunk was seen twice at Newfound Gap during September 1944 (Stupka, 1944).

Chipmunks are omnivorous and often use their large cheek pouches to carry food to storage places. Food items include nuts such as acorns, beechnuts, and chestnuts (formerly); small seeds; berries; wild grapes; and a variety of small animal life. In March 1935 near Bull Cave, a pile of opened land snails was found at the entrance to a chipmunk burrow (Fleetwood, 1935). Odum (1949), in a review of the mammals of Highlands, North Carolina, reported seeing a chipmunk attacking a young New England cottontail (*Sylvilagus transitionalis*).

Like other small mammals, the Eastern Chipmunk has many enemies. It may be captured by snakes, hawks, owls, foxes, bobcats, house cats, and weasels (Hamilton, 1943). In September 1943 Park Ranger Morrell came upon a timber rattlesnake (*Crotalus horridus*) that had just struck an adult female chipmunk (Stupka, 1943). A large timber rattlesnake killed in July 1949 near Pin Oak Gap (4500 ft.) contained the remains of one of these mammals (Stupka, 1949). Savage (1967) reported finding the remains of chipmunks in four timber rattlesnakes. A chipmunk was also found in a black rat snake (*Elaphe obsoleta*) taken in the Greenbrier area (Huheey and Stupka, 1967).

Illustration Number 9

EASTERN GRAY SQUIRREL
Sciurus carolinensis

The Eastern Gray Squirrel is a familiar sight in the Great Smokies, especially at the lower altitudes. Unlike the Eastern Chipmunk (*Tamias striatus*), this species spends most of its time in trees, coming to the ground mainly to find food.

These squirrels prefer to live in deciduous forests, especially oak and beech woods. Although they have been seen at all elevations in the Park, they are rare in the spruce-fir zone. These mammals have been observed on numerous occasions in such representative localities as Twentymile Creek, Cosby (1750 ft.), Cades Cove (1750–1800 ft.), Greenbrier (1700–2000 ft.), Smokemont, Cataloochee, Spence Field (4800 ft.), and Mt. Sterling. During a period of many years, only two individuals have been seen on Mt. Le Conte.

The Eastern Gray Squirrel is diurnal, foraging for food in the early morning and late afternoon. It is active throughout the year, and Palmer (1954) stated that, during the winter, dens in tree cavities may be occupied by several individuals at the same time. In the Park on January 24, 1935, four of these squirrels were found in a den in a dead chestnut tree (Fleetwood, 1935).

Palmer (1954) noted that in the Southeast there are two breeding seasons, in December or January and in late May, the gestation period being about 44 days. Nursing females have been reported on March 11 (Komarek and Komarek, 1938), May 15 (Stupka, 1937), August 28 (Stupka, 1944), and October 2 (Stupka, 1944). Two males in breeding condition and two half-grown individuals were taken in October by the Komareks. Half-grown young have also been seen in mid-April (Stupka, 1937).

There are occasional reports of all white or all black individuals, melanism being fairly common in more northern areas. On October 31, 1958, an albino Eastern Gray Squirrel was collected on the south shore of Fontana Reservoir, opposite Forney Creek (Stupka, 1958). A melanistic individual was seen by Fleetwood near Parson Bald on March 26, 1935.

Various types of nuts and fruits form the bulk of the diet of this squirrel, including acorns, walnuts, beechnuts, berries of American holly, chestnuts (formerly), and the fruits of dogwood, silverbell, buckeye, and American hornbeam trees. In February and March, squirrels have been seen cutting the flowering twigs of sugar maple, oak twigs with flowers and young leaves, pine twigs, and red maple twigs with bursting buds.

Squirrel populations are known to fluctuate over the years, a phenomenon which may be regulated by a combination of overpopulation and scarcity of food. In former times, the American chestnut was the main food item of these animals. As the chestnuts began disappearing, the squirrels began relying more heavily upon acorns. In some years, however, the oak trees do not bear fruit. Such was the case in 1946, and many animals emigrated from the Park in search of food. Mortality from starvation and hunting pressure was estimated to be 90% for some of the watersheds (Stupka, 1960b). During 1946, squirrels were seen swimming across Fontana Reservoir, and many were killed by cars along Park roads. In 1947, these mammals were extremely scarce, but by 1953 there was a large population in Cataloochee.

The Eastern Gray Squirrel has few enemies, although, in the Park, several are killed by motor vehicles every year. In July 1937, a squirrel identified as *Sciurus* sp. was found in the stomach of a large timber rattlesnake (*Crotalus horridus*) taken on Mt. Sterling Bald (5800 ft.) (Huheey and Stupka, 1967). Savage (1967) reported finding squirrels (*Sciurus* sp.) in five timber rattlesnakes. On June 24, 1951, at Cataloochee, an adult Eastern Gray Squirrel was removed from the stomach of another timber rattlesnake (Stupka, 1951). A bobcat (*Lynx rufus*), found dead along the transmountain road (2600 ft., North Carolina) on December 6, 1953, had eaten one of these squirrels (Stupka, 1953).

Illustration Number 10

EASTERN FOX SQUIRREL
Sciurus niger

This species, our largest squirrel, can be considered scarce or even rare in the Park. A heavy-bodied squirrel with a squarish facial profile, it can be recognized by its rusty brown color and by its blackish head, which contrasts sharply with its white nose. No specimens were taken by the Komareks, but, based on information from residents, they determined that these squirrels were common in certain localities adjacent to the Park. In 1936, Park Warden Sutton reported that the Eastern Fox Squirrel "occurs but is uncommon" in the vicinity of Walnut Bottoms.

These animals have been observed up to 4000 ft. elevation in the Park. There have been reports of fox squirrels in the following areas: Bradley Fork (about 2500 ft.); along Little River Road between Park Headquarters and Fighting Creek Gap; between Eagle and Hazel creeks (near Proctor); near Shuckstack Tower (4000 ft.); and at Wears Cove near the Park boundary.

Like other squirrels, the Eastern Fox Squirrel feeds upon nuts and fruits. An individual seen along Bradley Fork on July 6, 1940, was eating mulberries (Stupka, 1940).

RED SQUIRREL
Tamiasciurus hudsonicus

The Red Squirrel may be regarded as common to abundant in the Park. Locally known as "mountain boomer," this species reaches the southern limit of its range in northern Georgia. These squirrels are uniformly reddish, being paler on the back in the winter and having a black line along the side in the summer.

Red Squirrels have been observed at all elevations in the Park. During the warmer months of the year they are most plentiful in the spruce-fir region, whereas low-altitude records are especially numerous during the winter months. Localities from which these squirrels have been recorded include Park Headquarters (1450 ft.), Sugarlands (1800 ft.), Deep Creek, Smokemont, Greenbrier, Cosby, Cataloochee, Mt. Kephart, Newfound Gap, Clingmans Dome (6400 ft.), Mt. Guyot (6500 ft.), and Mt. Le Conte (6593 ft.). Two melanistic specimens were seen near Cosby in 1934.

As noted previously, squirrel populations may fluctuate considerably. David Ogle of Pigeon Forge, Tennessee, reported that he shot 47 Red Squirrels in two hours at Indian Gap in the 1890's. These mammals were also abundant in 1937 and 1938. In December 1937 Stupka counted 25 individuals between Greenbrier Pinnacle and Mt. Le Conte, a distance of 5 miles. Red Squirrels were scarce in 1939, 1940, and 1941.

Red Squirrels breed during the spring and summer, occasionally having two litters annually. On October 9, the Komareks noted a half-grown individual. The nest, constructed of shredded bark and other vegetation, is usually located in a natural tree cavity or a wood-pecker hole (Palmer, 1954). On May 24, 1952, Stupka observed one of these squirrels stripping thin bark from a yellow birch tree (*Betula alleghaniensis*) along the Appalachian Trail near Charlies Bunion. The squirrel proceeded to stuff its mouth full of bark and then ran off.

On August 22, 1955, a nest containing six young Red Squirrels was found in a hollow limb of a large yellow birch at approximately 4500 ft. along the transmountain road (Tennessee). The young squirrels were less than half the size of adults and had proportionately large heads and feet. Three of the young were adopted by Park Ranger John Morrell, who took them to his home in their nest of thin, yellow birch bark. The young squirrels grew rapidly on their diet of condensed milk and warm water four times a day. On the third day, one individual had its eyes open and, on the following day, the eyes of the other two were open. According to Palmer (1954), this would indicate that the squirrels were 23 or 24 days old at the time of their capture, and the date of their birth would be approxi-mately the last day of July. Apparently, this represents a second lit-ter. By November 10, two of the three animals had died. On that day the remaining squirrel, named Rufus, was liberated at the lower edge of the spruce-fir forest, a few miles from where he was born. This animal had lived with the Morrells for a period of 80 days. The story of Rufus does not end here, however. From November 23, 1955, to January 6, 1957—a period of more than 13 months—Mr. Morrell revisited 42 times the place where Rufus had been liberated. On 34 of these occasions, contact was made between man and squir-rel. Mr. Morrell would call the animal's name, and ordinarily in a matter of some minutes the squirrel would put in his appearance. Usually he accepted food from the hand of his benefactor. A second Red Squirrel occasionally accompanied Rufus on visits beginning January 22, 1956. On July 1, 1956, both squirrels accepted food from Mr. Morrell. Final contact was made on January 6, 1957, after which Rufus could not be located.

In the Park, Red Squirrels have been observed feeding on a variety of foods including the fruits of the cucumber-tree (*Magnolia acumi-nata*), mountain holly (*Ilex montana*), silverbell (*Halesia carolina*), beech (*Fagus grandifolia*), buckeye (*Aesculus octandra*), service-berry (*Amelanchier* sp.), black walnut (*Juglans nigra*), and Ameri-can chestnut (*Castanea dentata*); seeds of mountain maple (*Acer spicatum*), eastern hemlock (*Tsuga canadensis*), and various species of pine; cones of fir and spruce; mushrooms; the buds of the great white rhododendron (*Rhododendron maximum*); and garbage from roadside cans. The Komareks observed individuals feeding upon blackberries (*Rubus* sp.) and the buds of the buckeye (*Aesculus octandra*). In April 1938 Stupka saw a squirrel feeding on the sap of the yellow birch (*Betula alleghaniensis*). In 1952, an individual was found near Newfound Gap eating a nestling red-breasted nuthatch (*Sitta canadensis*) (Grimes, 1952).

Although preyed upon by a number of different animals in the Park, only two specific instances of predation have been recorded. In both cases the remains of a Red Squirrel were found in the stomach of a timber rattlesnake (*Crotalus horridus*)—one at Sheep Pen Gap (Tanner—personal communication to Stupka, 1949) and the other at Mt. Sterling Bald (Stupka, 1939).

SOUTHERN FLYING SQUIRREL
Glaucomys volans

The Southern Flying Squirrel is a common resident of the Park at the lower altitudes. This species can often be distinguished from its northern relative by the color of the belly hairs, which are entirely white (the base of these hairs is gray in the Northern Flying Squirrel).

This squirrel has been recorded at elevations ranging from 1800 ft. (Cades Cove) to 4700 ft. (Snake Den Mountain). It prefers to live in forested situations and has been taken in deciduous and mixed woodlands (Komarek and Komarek, 1938). Although seldom seen, it has been recorded at Abrams Branch, Big Creek, Deep Creek (2200 ft.), Greenbrier (2500 ft.), Smokemont (3000 ft.), Walnut Bottoms (3100 ft.), and Blanket Mountain.

These squirrels are nocturnal and may be active throughout the year. However, several individuals may congregate and sleep during periods of intense cold (Palmer, 1954). In December 1940, 26 of these mammals were found in one hollow chestnut tree (Stupka, 1960b). Active individuals have been seen in the Park during December and January.

In the South, this flying squirrel produces two litters a year—in early March and late August (Hamilton, 1943). A female collected on August 4, 1937, in Cades Cove contained four nearly full-term embryos.

Predators of this mammal in the Park are known to include snakes. A specimen was removed from the stomach of a timber rattlesnake (*Crotalus horridus*) taken near Gatlinburg in August 1960 (Stupka). Within a 24-hour period—May 15–16, 1953—Stupka prevented three black rat snakes (*Elaphe obsoleta*) from entering a bluebird house in which flying squirrels resided. After this incident, which occurred near his home close to the Park boundary, the squirrels disappeared.

Illustration Number 11

NORTHERN FLYING SQUIRREL
Glaucomys sabrinus

This flying squirrel, an uncommon inhabitant of the Park, was first discovered there on February 20, 1935, when a specimen was taken on Blanket Mountain (4000 ft.). Additional individuals have been noted along Walker Prong and at Newfound Gap. This species was never seen on Mt. Le Conte in the many years that J. Huff operated Le Conte Lodge.

Handley (1953) stated that this squirrel is "irregularly distributed at high elevations in the spruce and balsam cloud forests of the southern Appalachian Mountains." The specimen from Blanket Mountain, however, was found in a deciduous forest, "at least seven airline miles from the nearest spruce and fir" (Handley, 1953).

The Northern Flying Squirrel produces two litters annually, in spring and mid-summer (Hamilton, 1943). On August 22, 1959, a nursing female was found near Walker Prong. Usually, the shredded bark nest of this species is built in a tree cavity, often a woodpecker hole (Hamilton, 1943). However, on May 22, 1946, an outside nest, which was somewhat smaller than a football, was found in a dense spruce tree at 5000 ft. near Alum Cave Bluffs (Stupka). Considering the habitat and elevation, it is likely that the nest was constructed by this species and not by the Southern Flying Squirrel.

Beavers

FAMILY CASTORIDAE

The Beaver is the largest native North American rodent, often attaining a weight of 40 or 50 pounds or more. Its most distinguishing characteristic is its broad flat tail with which it slaps the surface of the water whenever it becomes alarmed. Signs indicating Beaver presence include the familiar dams, lodges, canals, and tree cuttings.

BEAVER
Castor canadensis

Although this species was widespread in former times, there had been no evidence of its occurrence within the area now encompassed by the Park until 1966. In 1896, Rhoads stated: "It is not likely that any beavers now exist in the eastern half of the State [Tennessee]." In discussing the status of the Beaver in North Carolina, Brimley (1945) stated that it was "apparently extinct," being last recorded from Stokes County about 1897. Hamnett and Thornton (1953) noted that it was exterminated throughout North Carolina by the early 1900's.

In 1962, a colony of Beavers was found inhabiting Alarka Creek, a few miles southwest of Bryson City, Swain County, North Carolina. Alarka Creek flows into Fontana Reservoir approximately 3 miles south of the Park boundary. In April 1966, Beaver dams were discovered in a small branch of Eagle Creek within the Park boundary (Park News and Views, 1966). On April 7, 1968, a Beaver was seen near the mouth of Pinnacle Creek on Eagle Creek; others were observed along the lower reaches of Hazel Creek (Park News and Views, 1968). Both localities are well within the Park boundary in Swain County, North Carolina. The occurrence of Beaver in the Park area is probably the result of introductions made in western North Carolina by the North Carolina Fish and Game Department.

Illustration Number 12

Native Rats and Mice

FAMILY CRICETIDAE

This family includes a vast number of extremely variable species. It is divided into two subgroups—one having large ears, large eyes, and long tails and another with small eyes, small ears, and short tails. The Park is inhabited by 14 of these rodents, which range in size from the Eastern Harvest Mouse (*Reithrodontomys humulis*) to the Muskrat (*Ondatra zibethicus*).

The habitats of the various forms differ considerably. Of the species in the Park, the majority dwell in fields or woodlands, but one form is aquatic (Muskrat) and another is semi-arboreal (Golden Deermouse—*Ochrotomys nuttalli*).

Most of these mammals are nocturnal, although some species are active during the day. None of them is known to hibernate.

This group is characterized by diverse food habits, but all are essentially omnivorous (Hamilton, 1943). Predators are many; these mammals often form the bulk of the diet of larger animals.

RICE RAT
Oryzomys palustris

The inclusion of the Rice Rat as a member of the Park fauna is based on the discovery of one individual, an immature female that was taken by the Komareks at Greenbrier (2200 ft.) on April 3, 1931. Although further work was done in this area in subsequent years, no additional specimens were obtained. Howell (1909) recorded seven specimens from the foot of the Cumberland Mountains of eastern Kentucky and Tennessee. Specific localities included Barbourville, Kentucky; High Cliff, Campbell County, Tennessee; Lawrenceburg, Tennessee; and Arlington, Shelby County, Tennessee.

Hamilton (1943) indicated that the Rice Rat is found wherever there is considerable ground cover of grass and sedges, particularly in wet meadows and marshy areas. The Greenbrier specimen was found dead on the sill of an old barn situated near a marshy creek.

In discussing their discovery, Komarek and Komarek (1938) stated: "This record is unique in that there seem to be no records of this species occurring above 1000 feet. Its distribution was apparently extended into the mountains as a result of agricultural activities of local residents."

Authorities disagree as to the range of this species. Hall and Kelson (1959) depict the range as not extending over the Park area, whereas Palmer (1954) and Burt and Grossenheider (1952) indicate that it does. However, Hall and Kelson state that the "northern limit of range of this species seems to fluctuate, probably owing to fluctuation of population densities and is less precisely known than for most common North American mammals."

EASTERN HARVEST MOUSE
Reithrodontomys humulis

The Eastern Harvest Mouse is similar in appearance to the House Mouse but has a somewhat hairier tail. Also, a close examination of the upper incisors reveals that there is a deep longitudinal groove in each tooth. This species has been said to be "locally distributed in a few isolated places" in the Great Smoky Mountains National Park (Komarek and Komarek, 1938).

This mouse has been found in the Park up to 1500 ft. elevation. The Komareks obtained seven individuals from Sevier County, Tennessee. Six of these were taken in small cleared areas under apple trees in a moderately overgrown broomsedge field, while the seventh was collected near a small hole leading under a rock in a similar field situation along Laurel Branch in Greenbrier. No other specimens have been recorded from the Park.

Although little is known concerning reproduction in the Eastern Harvest Mouse, Hamilton (1943) stated that breeding commences in March, and pregnant females have been taken as late as December. On October 18 the Komareks found a female which had enlarged mammary glands.

This species feeds on a variety of small seeds. The stomach of one individual examined by the Komareks contained unidentified seeds.

WOODLAND DEERMOUSE
Peromyscus leucopus

LONG-TAILED DEERMOUSE
Peromyscus maniculatus

The Woodland and Long-tailed Deermice are probably the most numerous mammals in the Park. These species appear identical to all but the experienced observer and, for this reason, they are combined in this discussion. To the naturalist, the Woodland Deermouse can usually be distinguished by its shorter, uniformly colored tail, in contrast to the longer, sharply bicolor tail (dark above, white below) of the Long-tailed Deermouse.

The Woodland Deermouse is especially abundant at the lower altitudes but has been recorded as high as 4500 ft. in the Park. The Long-tailed Deermouse is more common at the higher elevations and has been taken between 1400 and 6300 ft. elevation. In the Park, it has been found that the two species come together at about 3000 ft., although there is considerable overlap (Komarek and Komarek, 1938). This altitudinal division is also evident in areas surrounding the Park. In the Highlands, North Carolina, area, Odum (1949) found that the dividing line was 3400 ft. Of 73 Long-tailed Deermice taken by Barbour (1951) at Big Black Mountain, Kentucky, 67 were collected above 3000 ft. and none was found below 2700 ft. He also trapped 47 Woodland Deermice, 29 of which were taken below 2700 ft.

It has been noted that these two species tend to occupy different habitats but, as is the case with elevation, there are many areas where both are found. Howell and Conaway (1952) collected both species at the same station in the Cumberland Mountains, Tennessee. In a later paper (Conaway and Howell, 1953) dealing with the mammals of extreme northeastern Tennessee and adjacent areas in North Carolina, they stated that the Long-tailed Deermouse was "usually taken in cool and moist situations," while the Woodland Deermouse "was taken at lower elevations and in more open types of woods . . . ." Barbour (1951) noted that both species occupy the same habitat about the summit of Big Black Mountain, but as the elevation decreased, the Long-tailed Deermouse became less abundant and the Woodland Deermouse more numerous. In the Park, D. W. Pfitzer collected the two species at Moore's Spring Shelter within a few yards of each other.

The authors found some indication of a seasonal difference in the distribution of these two species. In March 1964, the Long-tailed Deermouse was observed along Cosby Creek (1720 ft.); during the summers of 1963 and 1964, however, no individuals of this species were found in this locality. Instead, Woodland Deermice occupied the area and were recorded at the same stations that previously yielded Long-tailed Deermice.

Breeding in both species commences in early spring and may continue well into fall (Hamilton, 1943). The Komareks examined female Long-tailed Deermice containing embryos on February 21, March 31, and August 24. The authors noted numerous females that were either pregnant or had recently given birth in February, March, April, July, August, September, and December. Males examined during March, July, September, and December were in breeding condition. A nest of the Woodland Deermouse containing four half-grown young was found in a register box at Chimneys Campground on October 31, 1960. From June to September 1963, numerous pregnant and nursing females and males in breeding condition were examined by the authors in the Cosby area.

Partly because they are so abundant, these deermice have innumerable enemies. Many instances of predation have been recorded in the Park. Three timber rattlesnakes (*Crotalus horridus*) taken near Gregory Bald, Trillium Gap, and Laurel Creek had eaten these mice (Stupka, 1945; 1947; 1954). Savage (1967) recorded deermice (*Peromyscus* sp.) from 21 timber rattlesnakes. The stomachs of two screech owls (*Otus asio*) found at the Tremont Y and near Park Headquarters contained remains of deermice (Stupka, 1938; 1949). A long-tailed weasel (*Mustela frenata*) seen on Mt. Le Conte near Le Conte Lodge was carrying a deermouse, and a specimen was removed from the stomach of a bobcat (*Lynx rufus*) killed along the transmountain road in Tennessee (Stupka, 1952). It can be stated with reasonable certainty that all of these predators had taken either the Woodland or Long-tailed Deermouse and not one of the other deermice found in the Park because of the abundance and wide distribution of these two species.

Long-tailed Deermouse, *Illustration Number 13*

COTTON DEERMOUSE
Peromyscus gossypinus

The Cotton Deermouse, or Cotton Mouse, is the largest and heaviest deermouse found in the Park. It is fairly common at the lower elevations.

This mouse has been taken in the Park between 1400 and 2800 ft. elevation. Areas where this species is found include Roaring Fork (1400 ft.), near Park Headquarters (1500 ft.), Fighting Creek near Gatlinburg, Little River at The Sinks (1565 ft.), Cades Cove (1750 ft.), Cosby, Laurel Creek (1800 ft.), and Greenbrier (1800–2800 ft.). The Komareks stated that it was frequently found "in the open woodlands and field margins at low elevations where farming activity has produced brush growth and open forest situations." This species is often taken in association with the Woodland Deermouse (*Peromyscus leucopus*), which it closely resembles. In Texas, when these two species occur in the same general area, the Woodland Deermouse is generally restricted to the uplands, while the Cotton Deermouse is found in the lowlands (McCarley, 1954). Observations by the authors during two summers in the Cosby area indicate that these two species are somewhat segregated by their habitat preferences. The Cotton Deermouse was most often observed in a low floodplain along Cosby Creek (1720 ft.), whereas the Woodland Deermouse was found mainly on higher ground considerably above the creek.

The Cotton Deermouse may breed throughout the winter (Hamilton, 1943). The Komareks collected two females on March 4, each containing three embryos, and found a male in breeding condition in October. A nursing female was recorded on August 26, 1963, by the authors, who also noted males in breeding condition during August, September, and October.

GOLDEN DEERMOUSE
Ochrotomys nuttalli

The most distinctive and unusual deermouse in the Great Smoky Mountains National Park is the Golden Deermouse. The common name of this mouse comes from its bright golden fur. It is unusual in that it is a semi-arboreal species, spending considerable time in trees and vines. Due to its arboreal habits, this species possesses several unique adaptations, such as a semi-prehensile tail and small feet. Although infrequently seen, it is not rare but occurs in highly localized populations. The ecology, home range, and habits of this species in the Park have been the subject of intensive study by the authors.

The Golden Deermouse has been recorded in the Park at elevations ranging up to 2700 ft. Areas include Deep Creek, The Sinks, Greenbrier (1680 ft.), Big Creek (1700 ft.), Cosby (1750–2500 ft.), Smokemont, Couches Creek, Fighting Creek, Cherokee Orchard (2500 ft.), and along Little River above Elkmont (2700 ft.). Stupka observed individuals in the Buckhorn area, near the Park boundary (Stupka, 1953). Nests have been recorded from Cataloochee, Deep Creek, Greenbrier, and Cosby.

The Komareks found these mice along the edges of broomsedge fields, brier patches, and old fences. Odum (1949) collected this mouse largely in forests and forest edges with heavy undergrowth, although one was taken in a rhododendron thicket located in a virgin hemlock tract. In the Cosby area, a large population of Golden Deermice has been intensively studied by the authors. These mice live in an area generally dominated by pine but having an extensive undergrowth of greenbrier (*Smilax* sp.). Several individuals at Cosby have also been found living in an area dominated by a dense growth of mountain laurel (*Kalmia latifolia*). At Deep Creek, however, the habitat consists mainly of deciduous trees with an understory of honeysuckle (*Lonicera* sp.).

Until recently, very little information has been available concerning the breeding habits of Golden Deermice. They generally build spherical nests 6 to 8 inches in diameter that may be located from a few inches to approximately 20 feet above the ground. These nests are usually located in tangles of greenbrier against the trunk of a tree. A detailed discussion of the composition and contents of 44 nests of this species found in the Park is presented by Linzey (1966; 1968). The breeding season of the Golden Deermouse in the Park extends from mid-March to early October, with peaks occurring in late spring and early fall (Linzey, 1966; Linzey and Linzey, 1967b). In the Park, a nest was found along Couches Creek on August 3, 1934, which contained a female and three blind hairless young. The Komareks collected a female on October 12 that appeared to have just finished nursing. A discussion of the changes that occur in the coat of this species at different ages and during different seasons of the year is presented by Linzey and Linzey (1967a).

The seeds of cherry (*Prunus*), dogwood (*Cornus*), and greenbrier (*Smilax*) were most frequently found in an examination of 44 Golden Deermouse nests. Greenbrier seeds, blackberry (*Rubus*) seeds, and insects were the most frequent food items identified in the stomachs and intestinal tracts of 54 individuals of this species. For a more detailed and complete analysis of the food items eaten by this species, see Linzey (1966; 1968).

Illustration Number 14

COMMON COTTON RAT
Sigmodon hispidus

The Common Cotton Rat, although abundant near Knoxville, Tennessee (Komarek and Komarek, 1938), and throughout the Southern states, is rare in the Great Smoky Mountains National Park. It has been recorded from only four localities Greenbrier (1700 ft.), Big Creek (1700 ft.), Cades Cove, and Mt. Sterling. Recently, three specimens have been collected near the Park. One was taken on March 20, 1960, at Gum Stand near Gatlinburg, and a second was found along Gnatty Branch near the Foothills Parkway on May 11, 1960. In August 1962 the authors collected a Common Cotton Rat in a field (2000 ft.) on the Cherokee Indian Reservation, Swain County, North Carolina, less than one-quarter of a mile east of the Park boundary.

Hamilton (1943) stated that this rat is found in broomsedge fields, roadside ditches, and the open glades of the forest to elevations of 1700 ft. The specimens from Greenbrier were taken by the Komareks in a heavily overgrown broomsedge field. They stated that its distribution was extended into the mountains as a result of agricultural activities. The individual taken at Big Creek was found in a swampy meadow (Fleetwood). Odum (1949) collected this rat in cultivated fields and hay meadows "up to at least 3200 feet elevation" in the Highlands, North Carolina, area.

Hamilton (1943) noted that "few mammals are more prolific" than the Common Cotton Rat. Although no breeding data are available from the Park, Odum (1949) recorded information from three females taken near Highlands in June 1948. One female contained nine well-developed embryos, while another had four small ones. A third individual was found to have given birth to 11 young.

EASTERN WOODRAT
Neotoma floridana

The Eastern Woodrat, once considered rare in this area, is now thought to be fairly common along the periphery of the Park. This species was not taken by the Komareks. The woodrat can be distinguished from other rats in the Park by its fairly long, well-haired (not scaly) tail.

These rats have been found in the Park from the lowest elevations up to 2500 ft. They were first recorded in 1936, when an individual was found dead along the Little River Road, one mile below The Sinks. Since then, specimens have been taken from a number of widely separated localities in the Park, including Abrams Creek Ranger Station (900 ft.), Happy Valley Ranger Station, Twentymile Creek, near The Sinks (1450 ft., 1565 ft.), Cades Cove, Chambers Creek—1½ miles above Fontana Reservoir—Big Creek (1600–1750 ft.), Sugarlands (1800 ft., 2000 ft.), Tremont (1925 ft.), and Cataloochee (2500 ft.).

Hamilton (1943) stated that "Rocky cliffs, caves and fissures or tumbled boulders on the sides of mountains are the preferred habitat" in Tennessee. Several woodrats have been found living in this type of habitat near The Sinks on the Little River. However, in the Park, many individuals and their nests have been discovered in and around old buildings. Rainey (1956) noted that in Kansas rock fences prepared in the process of clearing land for cultivation are frequently utilized by woodrats as homesites.

Information concerning the reproductive habits of the Eastern Woodrat is scarce, but breeding may occur irregularly throughout the year in the South (Hamilton, 1943). The nest of this species, constructed of shredded bark and grasses, is about the size of a football and shaped somewhat like a bird's nest. It is usually associated with a pile of debris, which may be up to 9 feet in diameter and 4 to 5 feet high (Rainey, 1956). Near Chambers Creek, a woodrat was frightened from a nest located 10 feet above ground in a dense growth of privet. On September 13, 1950, a nest found at Abrams Creek Ranger Station contained a nursing female and two blind young, approximately ten days old. Nursing females have also been taken on April 24, 1939, and August 14, 1950. A half-grown individual and two very small immature specimens were collected at Big Creek between October 1 and October 4, 1950.

The Eastern Woodrat is omnivorous, although Rainey (1956) noted that the bulk of its diet is vegetable matter such as berries, seeds, and grasses. Individuals taken in the Park in October 1950 had feasted on the berries of pokeweed (*Phytolacca* sp.). A woodrat found dead along the Little River Road on October 21, 1961, was holding in its mouth a sprig of poison ivy (*Rhus radicans*) with berries.

Although no specific data are available from the Park, Rainey (1956) stated that the black rat snake (*Elaphe obsoleta*), timber rattlesnake (*Crotalus horridus*), horned owl (*Bubo virginianus*), and spotted skunk (*Spilogale putorius*) are considered to be by far the most important natural enemies.

Illustration Number 15

SOUTHERN LEMMING MOUSE
Synaptomys cooperi

Since the Southern Lemming Mouse has seldom been recorded in recent years, it is difficult to determine its true status in the Park. These mice can be recognized by their short tails (less than 1 inch long), relatively massive heads, long fur, and upper incisor teeth that have a shallow groove near the outer edge of each tooth. Signs of this mouse, which consist of surface runways with small piles of grass cuttings, often reveal its presence. This species, also known as the Bog Lemming, reaches the southern limit of its range at Highlands, North Carolina (Odum, 1948a).

This small mammal has been found in the Park at elevations ranging from 1700 to 5500 ft., although records at the higher altitudes predominate. Although the Komareks noted 26 individuals of this species, only 8 have been recorded since 1934. The Komareks found individuals in "small, scattered grassy patches throughout the mountains." Typical localities frequented by this mouse in the Park include Roaring Fork, Greenbrier (1700 ft.), between Forney Creek and Jonas Creek (2400 ft.), Cataloochee, Kanati Fork (2800 ft.), Little River (2900 ft.), Grassy Patch (4000 ft.), Spence Field (5000 ft.), Indian Gap (5200 ft.), and Silers Bald (5400 ft., 5500 ft.). Odum (1949) collected this mouse at Highlands, North Carolina, in wet meadows, and, in one case, in a mass of wet sphagnum moss 6 inches below ground.

Hamilton (1943) remarked that in the mountains of North Carolina these mice breed from February to November. Females taken by the Komareks during March contained embryos (one to four) in various stages of development. The authors recorded two pregnant individuals in September and an immature mouse on October 31.

The food of the Southern Lemming Mouse consists mainly of green parts of low vegetation (Palmer, 1954). The stomachs of several individuals examined by Komarek and Komarek (1938) contained finely chewed grass.

Illustration Number 16

NORTHERN RED-BACKED MOUSE
Clethrionomys gapperi

The Northern Red-backed Mouse is common to abundant in the spruce-fir forests of the Great Smoky Mountains National Park and reaches its southern limit in the Highlands, North Carolina, area (Odum, 1949). In August 1950 Howell and Conaway (1952) took one individual in the Cumberland Mountains, the first record of this mouse in the mountains west of the Great Smokies.

These rather striking mice can be distinguished from all other mice in the Park by their wide reddish-brown back stripe and medium-length tail. They have been found at elevations ranging from 1750 to 6620 ft. in the Park. Representative areas they are known to inhabit include West Prong of the Little Pigeon River along the transmountain road (3400 ft., 4000 ft.), Low Gap (4242 ft.), Chapman Prong, Walker Prong, Bote Mountain (4700 ft.), Indian Gap (4800 ft., 5200 ft.), Silers Bald, Collins Gap (5800 ft.), Mt. Kephart, Clingmans Dome (6300–6400 ft.), and Mt. Guyot (6300–6620 ft.). The authors recorded one Northern Red-backed Mouse on Sutton Ridge near the Cosby Ranger Station (1750 ft.) and several from Kanati Fork (2800 ft.). These two localities represent the lowest elevations at which this species has been known to occur in the Park. Odum (1949) did not find this species below 3600 ft. in the Highlands, North Carolina, area. However, Paul and Quay (1963) recorded a mouse at 2750 ft. in the Toxaway River Gorge.

In humid forests, the Komareks frequently found these mice among mossy rocks, but specimens were also taken at the bases of isolated shrubs on top of a grassy bald (Spence Field). The authors collected these animals in a deciduous woodland. Odum (1949) noted that these mice were largely, if not entirely, restricted to moist forests, especially the coniferous forest communities. They were commonly found along small boulder-strewn streams and in rhododendron thickets.

The Northern Red-backed Mouse breeds from spring until fall. During the latter half of July, the Komareks examined two females containing three and four embryos, respectively. They also collected half-grown individuals on July 31 and August 23. On July 17, 1963, the authors noted a female with three embryos, two individuals containing two embryos apiece, and a nursing female that had recently given birth to four young. A pregnant female has also been taken in April and nursing females have been collected in April and August. Males in breeding condition have been noted in July.

Although a host of animals may capture this species, only one specific instance of predation has been recorded in the Park. Savage (1967) recorded a Northern Red-backed Mouse from a timber rattlesnake (*Crotalus horridus*). Barbour (1951) found individuals in the stomachs of four out of eight timber rattlesnakes examined at Big Black Mountain, Harlan County, Kentucky—approximately 80 miles north of the Great Smoky Mountains National Park.

Illustration Number 17

MEADOW VOLE
Microtus pennsylvanicus

Although Hall and Kelson (1959) indicated that the range of this species covered the Park area, and Odum (1948b) recorded its occurrence as far south as Georgia, the Meadow Vole was not taken in the Park until December 1965, when the authors recorded a juvenile female (Linzey and Linzey, 1967). This individual was found in a marshy field along the Oconaluftee River near the Smokemont Campground in North Carolina.

Runways believed to be those of this mouse had previously been reported along Forney Creek at the mouth of Jonas Creek by King in 1934 and on the Cherokee Indian Reservation near the Park boundary (Fleetwood).

YELLOW-NOSED VOLE
Microtus chrotorrhinus

Yellow-nosed Voles were first discovered in the Great Smoky Mountains National Park by Komarek (1932). These animals were found to represent a race new to science and are probably fairly common in areas above 3000 ft. elevation. These medium-sized mice are brownish, with some yellowish-brown or gray intermixed. The yellow or tawny snout may be obvious in some specimens, but may be inconspicuous or lacking in others.

The Yellow-nosed Vole has been found in the Park at elevations ranging from 2650 ft. to the summits of the highest mountains. The authors recorded this mouse along Indian Camp Creek (2650 ft.) and Kanati Fork (2800 ft.). The type specimen recorded by Komarek was taken along a tributary of Bradley Fork (3200 ft.) in Swain County, North Carolina. This mouse has also been found at Chimneys Campground, Smokemont (3200 ft.), Fort Harry Cliffs (3200 ft.), Eagle Rocks Creek (3800 ft.), Oconaluftee River (3800 ft.), Grassy Patch (4000 ft.), Buck Fork (4200 ft.), Spence Field (5000 ft.), Newfound Gap, Indian Gap (5200 ft.), Pecks Corner (5500 ft.), Thunderhead, Silers Bald, Andrews Bald (5800 ft.), and Mt. Kephart. The Komareks stated that this vole is generally distributed throughout the higher regions and is most common among the mossy rocks and logs in the high humid forest. On the grassy balds of Thunderhead they took several of these mice in rock outcrops. They noted that the vertical distribution corresponded with that of the Northern Red-backed Mouse (*Clethrionomys gapperi*) with which it shares the same habitat. In September and October 1950, individuals were noted by D. W. Pfitzer in three different types of habitat—a very rocky talus slope with no grasses, an open grassy area, and a birch-beech forest. The specimen recorded by the authors from Indian Camp Creek was obtained among mossy rocks and logs, while the specimen from Kanati Fork was taken amid scattered rocks along the stream.

Hamilton (1943) noted that the young are born from early spring well into the fall. The Komareks examined a female with three nearly full-term embryos on March 13. A pregnant female with four embryos has been taken on April 29, and nursing females have been noted on March 31 and April 29. Males in breeding condition have been collected in March, July, and August. In May 1947, Stupka noted a one-third grown individual on Andrews Bald. Immature individuals have also been taken in July, August, September, and October.

The food of this mouse includes small rootstocks, green grasses, fresh shoots, and berries (Hamilton, 1943). The stomach of one individual taken in the Park in September by the Komareks yielded blackberry seeds.

Several instances of predation on this vole have been recorded in the Park. In August 1952, a bobcat (*Lynx rufus*) was killed by a car along the transmountain road (3700 ft., Tennessee) and, upon examination, was found to contain five Yellow-nosed Voles. Savage (1967) reported finding this species of mouse in the stomachs of eight timber rattlesnakes (*Crotalus horridus*) and one copperhead (*Agkistrodon contortrix*).

Illustration Number 18

PINE MOUSE
Microtus pinetorum

The Pine Mouse is adapted to a life below ground and, like those of other semi-fossorial mammals, its eyes and external ears are reduced in size. Its thick, soft, short fur lies flat against the body whether rubbed forward or backward, an obvious adaptation for traveling either way in tunnels. It has a short tail and small, nearly concealed ears. This species is probably common in certain localities in the Park. The Komareks noted that it occurred in considerable numbers in some areas but was not generally common. Odum (1949) reported that these mice were locally common in one region at Highlands, North Carolina, and that single specimens were taken at widely scattered points.

Pine Mice have been found in the Park from the lowest elevations to 5000 ft., although the majority of records are below 2000 ft. At Cades Cove, the Komareks took specimens in an open deciduous woods where these mice had runways under a mat of dead leaves. They were also observed foraging about in the daytime in this locality. Specimens were collected at Greenbrier in an apple orchard and in a small marshy area at the edge of a woods (Komarek and Komarek, 1938). At Deep Creek, Pine Mice were found to inhabit a sedge field with pines on one side and oaks and shrubs on the other.

Odum (1949) trapped specimens in forest-edge situations. The authors have recorded this species from Cosby (1750 ft.), Cherokee Orchard (2400 ft.), and Cataloochee (2600 ft.). It has also been taken at Deep Creek (2000 ft.), Indian Creek (2000 ft.), Elkmont, and Spence Field (5000 ft.).

The Pine Mouse breeds from early March well into November and occasionally throughout the winter (Hamilton, 1943). Nursing females or females containing embryos have been recorded in March, September, and December. Males in breeding condition have been noted in September. An immature mouse was taken in March.

This mouse feeds largely on plant materials. The Komareks found pieces of grass, decomposed apples, and kernels of corn in the runways.

The semi-fossorial habits of this species may protect it from predators to some extent. A corn snake (*Elaphe guttata*) collected on December 16, 1937, in the Sugarlands area contained the remains of a Pine Mouse (Huheey and Stupka, 1967), and a copperhead (*Agkistrodon contortrix*) taken at Park Headquarters in August 1963 had also eaten one of these mice. Savage (1967) found this species in the stomachs of four copperheads. Barbour (1951) discovered an individual in the stomach of a black rat snake (*Elaphe obsoleta*) at Big Black Mountain, Kentucky-Virginia.

MUSKRAT
Ondatra zibethicus

These large rodents are fairly common in the Park in the larger streams at low altitudes. They rarely penetrate very deeply into the mountains but are generally restricted to the periphery of the Park. These animals have dense, rich brown fur overlaid with coarse outer hairs. The long, naked, black tail, which is flattened from side to side, is sufficient to distinguish the Muskrat from all other mammals in the Park.

Muskrats are known to occur up the Middle Prong of the Little Pigeon River to Greenbrier, at Cosby (2400 ft.), in the vicinity of Gatlinburg, and at Elkmont. In the western part of the Park, they have been found in Cades Cove (1800 ft.) and at the mouth of Abrams Creek. They also inhabit rivers on the North Carolina side and have penetrated 2 miles up Bradley Fork and the Oconaluftee

Illus. No. 1 (a). Opossum

Illus. No. 1 (b). Opossum (immature)

Illus. No. 2. Smoky Shrew

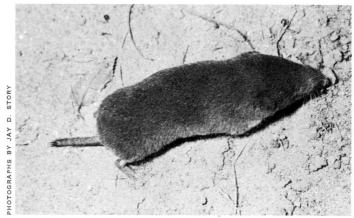

Illus. No. 3. Big Short-tailed Shrew

Illus. No. 4. Eastern Mole

Illus. No. 5. Red Bat

Illus. No. 6. Eastern Lump-nosed Bat

Illus. No. 7 (a). Eastern Cottontail

Illus. No. 7 (b). Eastern Cottontail (immature)

Illus. No. 9. Eastern Chipmunk

Illus. No. 10. Eastern Gray Squirrel

Illus. No. 11 (a). Southern Flying Squirrel

Illus. No. 11 (b). Southern Flying Squirrel

Illus. No. 12. Beaver

Illus. No. 13. Long-tailed Deermouse

Illus. No. 14. Golden Deermouse

Illus. No. 17. Northern Red-backed Mouse

Illus. No. 15. Eastern Woodrat

Illus. No. 18. Yellow-nosed Vole

Illus. No. 16. Southern Lemming Mouse

Illus. No. 19. Muskrat

Illus. No. 20. Woodland Jumping Mouse

Illus. No. 21. Red Fox

Illus. No. 22. Black Bear

Illus. No. 23. Raccoon

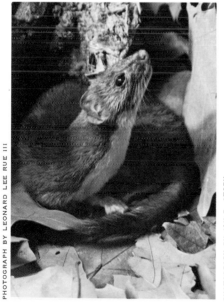

Illus. No. 24. Long-tailed Weasel

Illus. No. 25. Mink

Illus. No. 26. Spotted Skunk

Illus. No. 27. Striped Skunk

Illus. No. 28. River Otter

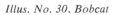

Illus. No. 29. Mountain Lion

Illus. No. 30. Bobcat

Illus. No. 31. European Wild Boar

Illus. No. 32. White-tailed Deer

River. Muskrats also occur in Deep Creek, Forney Creek, and Indian Creek. Although generally found below 2400 ft., two individuals have been noted at unusually high elevations. In April 1949, a young Muskrat was seen on the Rainbow Falls Trail at 5300 ft. (Tanner—personal communication to Stupka, April 28, 1949), and an individual was found dead on the transmountain road (Tennessee) at 4500 ft. in March 1951 (Stupka). Perhaps these specimens represent wandering individuals.

Muskrats are chiefly vegetarians, although animal food may be included in the diet (Hamilton, 1943). The Komareks found these mammals feeding on the young shoots of willow (*Salix* sp.). Near Ravensford, North Carolina, a large patch of corn was destroyed by these mammals, and it has been suggested that the decrease in the number of corn fields in the Greenbrier area has had its effect on the Muskrat population. In January 1961 Stupka received a report that a stoneroller minnow (*Campostoma anomalum*) was captured and carried off by one of these rodents near Gatlinburg.

An albino Muskrat was found along Cosby Creek (2400 ft.) on August 29, 1961. This individual, which was between one-half and two-thirds grown, had snow-white fur and pink eyes.

Illustration Number 19

Old World Rats and Mice
FAMILY MURIDAE

These non-native mammals are seldom found far from the habitation of man. They can be distinguished from our native species by an examination of the tail, which is nearly devoid of hair. There are three species found in the Park and throughout North America.

These mammals are found wherever there is a sufficient supply of food and water. Rats are nocturnal, whereas the House Mouse (*Mus musculus*) may be active both day and night. These species remain active throughout the year. Rats and mice are extremely prolific, and, if conditions are favorable, they will breed throughout the year.

The diet of these rats and mice is quite varied. Much has been written about the economic importance of these mammals, but Hamilton (1943) summed up the situation when he said of the Brown Rat (*Rattus norvegicus*): "The rat is the greatest mammal pest of mankind. It has caused more deaths than all the wars of history." Fortunately, these species seem to have rapidly declined in the Park area, presumably due to its largely uninhabited condition.

BROWN RAT
Rattus norvegicus

The Brown Rat, which is also known as the Norway or House Rat, is found in the Park wherever an appreciable amount of garbage accumulates. Like the House Mouse (*Mus musculus*), it is more localized and less abundant than in pre-Park days due to a more limited food supply. The Brown Rat is distinguished by its sparsely haired, scaly tail, which is shorter than the combined length of the head and body, and by its grayish brown color.

The Komareks found this rat most commonly around buildings and occasionally in rock fences bordering corn fields. They collected a specimen along Eagle Rocks Creek (3800 ft.), 5 miles from the nearest habitation. In July 1957, a half-grown individual was taken near a garbage can along Clingmans Dome Road at 6000 ft. (Stupka, 1957). Additional specimens have been taken at Gatlinburg (1300 ft.), Big Creek (1700 ft.), Greenbrier, and Elkmont (2500 ft.).

BLACK RAT
Rattus rattus

The Black Rat is an uncommon resident of the Great Smoky Mountains National Park. It differs from the Brown Rat in that its sparsely haired scaly tail is longer than the head and body. Although Komarek and Komarek (1938) reported that this species was abundant around barns at Greenbrier, it is probably much more scarce now than in former times. Paul and Quay (1963) recorded one specimen from the Toxaway River Gorge at an elevation of 1400 ft. It was found in an area which had been farmed 40 years previously but which had no evidences of habitation remaining in 1961.

In the Park, this rat has been recorded from a wide range of elevations. The Komareks collected three specimens at Greenbrier. Individuals have also been found at Park Headquarters, along Little River near Metcalf Bottoms (1800 ft.), Elkmont (2150 ft.), and Smokemont (2200 ft.). On July 24, 1941, one of these rats was taken on the summit of Mt. Le Conte (6300 ft.).

HOUSE MOUSE
Mus musculus

The House Mouse is a small grayish brown mouse with nearly hairless ears. The long, scaly, hairless tail is about the same color above and below. This species is probably much less common now than it was before the establishment of the Park due to a more limited supply of food and shelter.

The Komareks took this species most frequently around cabins and barns but stated that it is sometimes found at a considerable distance from human habitations. Barbour (1951), for example, trapped a House Mouse at 2600 ft. on Big Black Mountain (Kentucky-Virginia) one-half mile from the nearest human habitation. Individuals have been found as high as 2700 ft. and have been taken near Park Headquarters (1500 ft.), Greenbrier (1700 ft.), Cades Cove (1750 ft.), Forney Creek, Elkmont (2500 ft.), and near Low Gap (2700 ft.).

Jumping Mice
FAMILY ZAPODIDAE

Two representatives of this family occur in the Park—the Northern Meadow Jumping Mouse (*Zapus hudsonius*) and the Woodland Jumping Mouse (*Napaeozapus insignis*). These species may be considered among the most unusual mice inhabiting the Great Smoky Mountains National Park. They can readily be distinguished from other mice in the Park by their very large hind feet and long tails, features that render them similar to the unrelated kangaroo rats (*Dipodomys* sp.) of the West. Jumping mice also have grooves on the front surface of their upper incisors.

These mice are usually noctural and consequently are rarely seen. They are among our few true hibernators and may spend as much as six months of the year in their underground winter quarters. Hamilton (1943) described the hibernating position as follows: "the mouse curls in a tight ball, its head tucked under the body. The tail is curled like a watchspring."

These mice feed on a variety of seeds, berries, and grasses, as well as insects and other small invertebrate life.

NORTHERN MEADOW JUMPING MOUSE
Zapus hudsonius

One of the rarest mice inhabiting the Park is the Northern Meadow Jumping Mouse. This handsome creature has a very long bicolor tail and a pure white belly that contrasts sharply with its dark yellowish-brown sides. A dark brown stripe covers the back from nose to tail. It can usually be distinguished from the Woodland Jumping Mouse (*Napaeozapus insignis*) by the absence of the white tip on its tail.

As its name implies, this animal inhabits open, grassy areas. The absence of such areas and the fact that the Park lies near the southern boundary of its range (Petrides, 1948; Jenkins and Johnston, 1950; Golley, 1962) may account for the rarity of this mouse. Since Park lands are progressing toward a more forested condition, it seems certain that this animal will never become abundant.

The Northern Meadow Jumping Mouse has been recorded from only three areas in the Park. On November 7, 1935, several hibernating individuals were dug out of a loose clay bank along Noland Creek (approximately 2900 ft.). Each was located in a separate compartment (hibernaculum) lined with dry leaves, approximately 18 inches below ground level. On February 7, 1941, near Deep Creek (1750 ft.), a single hibernating mouse was found 4 to 6 inches below the surface of a clean road fill. These localities are in Swain County, North Carolina. The first recorded specimen from the Tennessee side of the Park was taken by the authors on August 3,

1964, at an elevation of 1720 ft. (Linzey and Linzey, 1966). This individual was found in an area of high weeds completely surrounded by deciduous woodlands, approximately 450 feet northeast of Cosby Creek near the Cosby Ranger Station.

Young jumping mice are born from early June to September or later (Palmer, 1954). Odum (1949) recorded a female that gave birth to four young on July 31. An individual taken near Athens, Georgia, produced a litter of six young near the end of September 1944 (Petrides, 1948).

WOODLAND JUMPING MOUSE
Napaeozapus insignis

The Woodland Jumping Mouse is not uncommon in the Park, but, rather than being of widespread distribution, it seems localized in certain areas. With its bright orange-brown sides and white tail tip, it is even more beautiful than its close relative, the Northern Meadow Jumping Mouse (*Zapus hudsonius*). The Woodland Jumping Mouse reaches the southern limit of its range in northern Georgia (Golley, 1962).

This mouse has been found at a wide range of elevations in the Park. It is at home along the rhododendron-covered shores of mountain streams but has also been taken near streams in dense woods with little or no underbrush. Localities this species is known to frequent include Park Headquarters (1600 ft.), Cosby (1750–2500 ft.), Big Creek (2200 ft.), Elkmont (2500 ft.), Chimneys Campground, Buck Fork (3000 ft.), Tremont (3200 ft.), Alum Cave Parking Area (3800 ft.), Grassy Patch (4000 ft.), Eagle Rocks Creek (4000 ft.), Walker Prong (4750 ft.), Appalachian Trail between Low Gap and Mt. Cammerer (4242–4850 ft.), Indian Gap (5200 ft.), and Forney Ridge (6300 ft.).

The Woodland Jumping Mouse may still be abroad in early winter. An active individual was taken along Cosby Creek (2500 ft.) on November 27, 1934. Several have been seen during late September and October. Usually, these mice do not emerge from hibernation until spring is well under way. However, on February 2, 1964, former Assistant Park Superintendent David deL. Condon observed an active individual near Park Headquarters.

The Woodland Jumping Mouse has three to six young in late

June or early July, and some individuals have a second litter in September (Hamilton, 1943). In the Cosby area, the authors have examined males in breeding condition in June, July, and August. They have also found nursing females in June, July, August, and September. At Highlands, North Carolina, Odum (1949) collected an individual containing four near-term embryos on June 21, 1948.

In the Park, these mammals are preyed upon by birds and snakes and by other mammals. Two timber rattlesnakes (*Crotalus horridus*) taken in the vicinity of the Tremont CCC Camp (3200 ft.) in October 1947 and along Kephart Prong (3000 ft.) during July 1951 had eaten these mice. Two mice were taken from the stomach of a rattlesnake found along the Little River above Elkmont in August 1963. Savage (1967) removed specimens from nine timber rattlesnakes. In October 1950 an individual was removed from the stomach of a screech owl (*Otus asio*) found near Smokemont (Stupka, 1950). A bobcat (*Lynx rufus*) found dead on the transmountain road (3700 ft.) in Tennessee in August 1952 contained the remains of six Woodland Jumping Mice (Stupka, 1952).

Illustration Number 20

Wolves and Foxes
FAMILY CANIDAE

Two members of this family, the Red Fox (*Vulpes fulva*) and the Gray Fox (*Urocyon cinereoargenteus*), presently occupy the Park. A third species, the Gray Wolf (*Canis lupus*), has become extinct in this area and now occurs in only a few areas in the United States.

Foxes are principally nocturnal, although they are frequently seen during the day. The Red Fox is found in diverse habitats, often near man, whereas the Gray Fox prefers to avoid civilization (Hamilton, 1943).

Mating in these forms occurs in late winter, and the young are usually born in March or April. Young Red Foxes remain with the parents until late summer, whereas the female Gray Fox separates from her young during the fall.

Foxes are omnivorous, feeding on small rodents, birds, snakes, turtles, berries, and insects. Man is probably the greatest enemy of these species in unprotected areas.

GRAY WOLF
Canis lupus [Extirpated]

The Gray Wolf, which once ranged widely throughout the United States, has been largely exterminated from many of its former habitats due to the activities of man. It once occurred in the Smokies in fair numbers, but it became increasingly less common as more of the land was settled.

The first mention of the status of wolves in this area came in 1844, when a letter to a member of the House of Representatives (Lanman, 1849) stated that sheep were destroyed by wolves, "which have not yet been entirely exterminated." In 1859, Buckley reported that wolves were "troublesome" to the mountain farmers of North Carolina and Tennessee.

In letters written to Stupka in 1952 and 1953, the late Dr. G. S. Tennent of Asheville related several instances of wolves in this area. Between 1876 and 1881, Dr. Tennent's brothers camped on the Pisgah Ridge while tending cattle and "after the advent of cool weather, they invariably spoke of hearing them [wolves]. . . ." On one occasion, Dr. Tennent met a hunter who told of a wolf raiding a flock of sheep along Pisgah Creek. In 1890, a wolf was killed in Cataloochee Township and another killed near Asheville, North Carolina. He also related that prior to the 1890's wolves were plentiful in the Cataloochee Mountains and in the wildest parts of the Balsams, but, with the coming of the railroad, they disappeared. Dr. Tennent concluded that "These facts would put the final disappearance of 'wolves' about the middle eighties, and leave the possibility of one or two strays hanging on into the present century." He related that the last Buncombe County (North Carolina) wolf was seen about 1890.

In 1887, C. H. Merriam (1888) noted that wolves "still occur" in the Great Smokies, and John Oliver, a former resident of the Park, remembered hearing wolves howling in Cades Cove when he was a boy (1880–1890). D. Ogle of Gatlinburg recalled seeing one of these animals that had been caught in a bear trap near the Sugarlands during the 1890's. He also heard two wolves howling near the area that is now Chimneys Campground.

Brimley (1944) wrote that wolves were "apparently finally exterminated in or about 1890, up to which time they still occurred sparingly in the mountains." Hamnett and Thornton (1953) stated: "In the Mountain Region . . . wolves existed in the more remote sections until the late 1800's and possibly until the very early 1900's."

There have been occasional unconfirmed reports of "wolves" in the mountains after 1900. The Asheville *Citizen-Times* published an account of an incident that took place in June 1903. This report related that a "pack of 75 or 100 fierce wolves were denned in Hangover Mountain [two miles west of Tapoco, North Carolina] just across the Tennessee River and often made raids upon sheep and cattle herds. Six years later [1909] the wolf pack was exterminated and with their passing the timber wolf became a legend in North Carolina." During the autumn of 1910, a "wolf" was reportedly heard and seen on Sinking Creek, a tributary of Big Creek, approximately two miles east of Mt. Guyot.

The most recent reported occurrence of the wolf in this area was related by the late G. S. Tennent of Asheville (personal communication to Stupka, August 21, 1953). A lone individual was killed by J. W. Parker, a patrolman for the Sherwood Forest Company near Waynesville, Haywood County, North Carolina, on February 27, 1933. An account of the incident, which occurred beyond Sunburst at Spruce in Cecil Township, was related by an Asheville, North Carolina, newspaper. The account stated that "this is the first time a wolf has been seen in Haywood County in about 40 years."

These reports of "wolves" since 1900 are included only for the purpose of giving a complete account of reported occurrences of this species. Official verification is lacking for all of these reports. Unqualified observers have been known to identify large dogs as wolves. Furthermore, since the Coyote has been extending its range eastward for many years, some of these observations may mistakenly refer to that species or to a hybrid coyote-dog (coydog). The Coyote, a smaller animal, carries its tail between its legs when running; a running wolf, however, carries its tail high.

RED FOX
Vulpes fulva

Although the Red Fox is an uncommon resident of the Great Smoky Mountains National Park, fox populations have been known to fluctuate, with peaks at nine- or ten-year intervals (Palmer, 1954). At Walnut Bottoms in June 1936, a ratio of one Red Fox to four Gray Foxes was estimated. Stupka (1938a) reported that these foxes were "present in fair numbers." The Red Fox can be distinguished from the Gray Fox by the white tip on its long bushy tail and by its black legs and feet.

The Red Fox has been observed at all elevations in the Park. Individuals have been recorded from Park Headquarters, Dudley Creek, Forney Creek, Straight Fork, near Metcalf Bottoms, Cosby, Walnut Bottoms, Becks Bald (4600 ft.), Spence Field (5000 ft.), Boulevard Trail, Indian Gap, and Mt. Le Conte.

Mating usually occurs in January and February, and the young foxes are born after a gestation period of approximately 52 days (Palmer, 1954). They are weaned in eight to ten weeks. On July 23, 1937, Stupka observed a two-thirds grown fox on the trail between Bryson Place and the state line. Two half-grown foxes were observed in the vicinity of Spruce Mountain on June 22, 1943 (Stupka), and an individual between two-thirds and three-quarters grown was found dead along the road near Metcalf Bottoms on September 21, 1951 (Stupka).

Food of the Red Fox includes cottontails, mice, insects, birds, turtles, snakes, carrion, and fruit (Hamilton, 1943). The stomachs of two specimens found by Stupka at Indian Gap and along the Boulevard Trail in December contained grasshoppers (*Schistocerca*). On September 12, 1944, seven freshly killed big short-tailed shrews (*Blarina brevicauda*) were noted along 1½ miles of the Appalachian Trail just prior to the observation of a Red Fox in that area by a group of hikers (Stupka).

Although the usual color of the Red Fox varies from bright reddish to pale tawny, variations occasionally occur. On December 17, 1934, a specimen that was "entirely black" was reported along Forney Creek Road.

There is some confusion as to whether the Red Fox is a native or an introduced member of the fauna of the southeastern United States. Audubon and Bachman (1846) stated that: "In the early history of our country the Red Fox was unknown south of Pennsylvania, that State being its Southern limit. In process of time it was found in the mountains of Virginia, where it has now become more abundant than the Gray Fox. A few years afterwards it appeared in the more elevated portions of North Carolina, then in the mountains of South Carolina, and finally in Georgia, where we have recently observed it."

However, Komarek and Komarek (1938) reported being informed that a number of foxes had been liberated in areas adjacent to the Park. In answer to a request for information, the following reply was received from Willis King, who was at that time Assistant Wildlife Technician of the National Park Service: "Mr. W. T. Griffiths and Homer Willicks, officials in the Association [Blount County, Tennessee, Fox Hunters Association], advised me that about 150 red foxes were liberated in Chilhowee Mountain from near Sevierville to the Tennessee River, during the years from 1924 to 1926. Points of liberation mentioned were Callahan, Montvale, Townsend, Walland, Allegheny and Chilhowee. The animals were shipped from Waterloo, Minnesota. According to their description, the animals are distinguishable from the native red fox in that they appear somewhat larger, are more yellowish and have more white on the face and tip of the tail. The legs were described as being less dark than those of the native animals. From this description it would appear that the introduced form may be the species *Vulpes regalis.*"

The issue is further confused by additional accounts. In discussing the mammals of Highlands, North Carolina, Odum (1949) stated that "there can be little doubt that the red fox is native to the region although not common." He acknowledged, however, that "it is possible that red foxes introduced into adjacent regions may have reached the [Highlands] Plateau, although there is no direct evidence." Hamnett and Thornton (1953) further debated this issue, stating that "although the red fox is not a native of North Carolina, he has been present in a few sections of North Carolina for many years, probably first appearing in the State in the northernmost mountain counties. Appearances of red foxes in this section were possibly due to early releases of these animals in Virginia since we have no records of releases in North Carolina at that time." Smith, Funderburg, and Quay (1960) noted that Red Foxes (*Vulpes fulva regalis*) from Minnesota, North Dakota, Iowa, and Nebraska were introduced in the mountains of North Carolina between 1953 and 1955. Finally, Golley (1962), remarking on the distribution of the Red Fox throughout the northern half of Georgia, stated that it was "probably introduced into the state for hunting purposes."

In all probability, the "native" animals (*Vulpes fulva*) discussed by King originally came to the Park from Virginia, either as a result of range extension or releases. Subsequently, "non-native" foxes (*Vulpes regalis*) released in Tennessee entered the Park.

Illustration Number 21

GRAY FOX
Urocyon cinereoargenteus

The Gray Fox is an abundant inhabitant of the Great Smoky Mountains National Park. Although the Komareks reported that this species "is said to be less common than the Red Fox," it is estimated at present that the Gray Fox outnumbers the Red Fox about five to one over the Park as a whole. In June 1936 the warden at Big Creek calculated that there were four Gray Foxes to every Red Fox. Odum (1949) reported that the Gray Fox was the common species in the Highlands, North Carolina, area. One of the best identifying features of this fox is its long, bushy, black-tipped tail, which has a median stripe along its entire length.

This species has been observed most frequently at the lower elevations. The highest recorded occurrence for this fox was near Newfound Gap. Representative localities include Park Headquarters, Big Creek, Cades Cove (1800–2000 ft.), Cooper Creek, Pilot Ridge, Smokemont, and Elkmont (2500 ft.).

The Gray Fox breeds during February and March (Palmer, 1954). Young foxes are born in March or April (Hamilton, 1943). On February 26, 1960, a copulating pair was seen near Park Headquarters (Stupka). A nursing adult female was found dead along the Cades Cove road on May 14, 1941 (Stupka), and a young male, weighing 9½ pounds, was found dead at Smokemont on October 30, 1939 (Stupka).

The Gray Fox is omnivorous and consumes a great variety of food items. Stomach contents of an individual found near Smokemont in August 1934 revealed grasshoppers (Acrididae and Locustidae), beetles (*Necrophorus, Eucanthus,* and *Pinetus*), pokeweed seeds (*Phytolacca decandra*), and a spider. Examination of an individual from near Townsend, Tennessee, on September 13, 1950, revealed

70% invertebrates and 30% vegetation (Pfitzer). A third fox found near Smokemont in late September 1950 was found to contain 95% camel crickets and 5% other insects and centipedes (Pfitzer). Other food items removed from stomachs of various individuals include acorns, maple seeds, persimmons, and various small mammals. The Gray Fox has been known to steal chickens, and it has been reported to prey upon wild turkeys.

The Gray Fox has few natural enemies. Some Gray Foxes are known to have been killed by automobiles along roads in and near the Park.

Bears

FAMILY URSIDAE

Four types of bears (Black, Grizzly, Big Brown, and Polar) inhabit the United States, but only the Black Bear occurs in the Great Smoky Mountains National Park. Bears are the largest living carnivores, with one species (Big Brown Bear) attaining a weight of 1,500 pounds or more. Although classified as carnivores, many of them also feed upon berries, nuts, and fruits.

BLACK BEAR
Ursus americanus

For the visitor to the Park, the most popular animal living in the area is undoubtedly the Black Bear, its largest native mammal. It is estimated that approximately 300 of these animals inhabit the Park, a figure which may seem far too conservative to those who see several while visiting the area. However, it must be remembered that the bears are concentrated near the campgrounds and along the highways during the summer.

The average adult Black Bear usually weighs between 200 and 300 pounds. One bear weighing 550 pounds and another weighing between 350 and 400 pounds have been recorded at Elkmont (Park News and Views, 1966; 1967). On October 17, 1959, a Black Bear with a field-dressed weight of 489 pounds was reported shot in the Chilhowee Mountains near the Park.

Bears occur throughout the Park at all elevations. Signs of their presence have been detected during every month of the year. Although the Black Bear is often thought of as a true hibernator, this is not technically correct. Its general metabolism is maintained at nearly normal levels during the colder months, and the animal merely enters a deep sleep. When cold winter temperatures descend upon the Park (middle and late December), a denning site is chosen. Typical examples of such sites are in hollow logs, under overhanging rock ledges, beneath fallen evergreen trees, or any other spot which will shelter the bear from the cold winds, rain, and snow. On March 31, 1947, a bear was found "sleeping" under large rocks along a tributary of Forney Creek (2800 ft.). When disturbed, it shifted its position but did not leave its bed (Stupka, 1947). Occasionally, the animal may emerge from its den and walk about for a short distance, leaving evidence of its mid-winter stroll in the snow. The bear generally returns to its den without eating anything.

Female Black Bears breed every second year, and the cubs are born in late January or February, while the female is still in her den. The number of cubs ranges from one to six, although two is most common. It is unusual to find four cubs, and litters of five or six have been recorded on very rare occasions (Rowan, 1945; 1947). During the summer of 1963, the authors noted two female bears, each of which had four cubs. One of these was observed in July near the Chimneys Parking Overlook on the transmountain road; the second bear frequented the Cosby Campground and was seen on many occasions. The latter bear, with two of the cubs, returned to the Cosby area during the summer of 1964. Newborn cubs are extremely small, weighing less than one pound apiece. They emerge from the den with the mother bear in late March or April. In the Park, the earliest observation of a newborn cub away from the den was between March 4 and 10, 1962, when an individual weighing between 5 and 10 pounds was seen several times in the Parsons Branch area. Another early observation was on April 8, 1960, when a cub weighing 5 pounds, 11 ounces was recorded at Metcalf Bottoms (Stupka, 1960b). The cubs remain with the parent for about a year and a half. Palmer (1954) states that after ten months, the young bears weigh between 30 and 80 pounds, with an average of 55 pounds. Few records of weights of cubs in the Park are available, however. A 24-pound cub was recorded on July 14, 1942, and on August 8, 1948, a 23-pound individual was noted. A 26-pound cub was observed on September 20, 1942 (Stupka). All three cubs were males. Very small cubs have been observed on two occasions—December 17, 1954, near Fighting Creek Gap and July 27, 1963, near Park Headquarters (Stupka). The life span of a wild Black Bear probably does not exceed 12 to 15 years (Palmer, 1954).

Although classified as a carnivore, bears are essentially omnivorous and vary their diet with the season. In the spring, they feed on the tender leaves of plants and on the deciduous mast that has lain on the ground during the winter (Komarek and Komarek, 1938). During summer and autumn, their diet is governed by the availability of ripening fruits. Foods known to be eaten by bears in the Park include blackberries, strawberries, blueberries, huckleberries, acorns, chestnuts, beechnuts, wild grapes, young beech leaves, persimmons, pokeweed berries, grasses, herbs, and the fruits of the sassafras, fire cherry, black gum, and mountain ash trees. They have also been known to consume garbage, wood-eating roaches, yellow jackets, carrion, poultry, and livestock. The availability of garbage (and occasionally food from picnic baskets) around the campgrounds and along the highways during the summer makes these favorite feeding places. From late July to October, there have been many records of bears raiding yellow jacket nests. Palmer (1954) reported that adult bears strip bark from the bases of conifers, eat its soft inner layer, and nibble the moist tree trunk. Trees other than conifers that have been chewed by Park bears include red maple, hickory, red oak, and yellow poplar.

In former times, the chestnut (*Castanea dentata*) was one of the main foods of the Black Bear. However, due to the fungus disease that has attacked this tree, essentially no large fruit-bearing chestnuts remain in the Park. As the number of these trees declined, acorns became important as a food item. Usually there is an abundant supply of acorns, but occasionally the oak trees fail to bear fruit. When this happens, as it last did in 1946 (Stupka, 1960b), the bears throughout the entire Southern Appalachian region face a food shortage. Large numbers of bears leave the protective confines of the Park to search for food in surrounding areas, where they may be taken by hunters. In 1946, it was estimated that the Park lost between one-third to one-half of its bear population.

Depredations by bears have been severe during certain periods. The superintendent's report for June 1932 stated: "Bears continue to kill sheep and hogs on the range in the Thunderhead and Gregory Bald sections." Bearproof storage for food was begun in June 1935 after several work camps in the Park suffered damage. For August 1944 the Park naturalist's monthly report to the superintendent mentioned a number of incidents of bears attacking cattle, pigs, and chickens as a result of the scarcity of wild foods; these were mostly in the immediate vicinity of the Park.

Illustration Number 22 and back cover

Raccoons
FAMILY PROCYONIDAE

Members of this family occur in the Americas, as well as in eastern Asia. The Raccoon is the most widespread Procyonid and is the only representative in the Park, although the family also includes such diverse forms as the ring-tailed cat, coati, kinkajou, and the pandas. In many of the species, facial markings are present, and, in most, the tail is ringed with light and dark bands.

RACCOON
Procyon lotor

The familiar Raccoon is one of the Park's more handsome mammals, with its black facial mask and black-ringed bushy tail. The fact that pelts were once used as barter in this area is evidence that the Raccoon has long been abundant (Kephart, 1921). Hunnicutt (1926) remarked that in pre-Park days he "helped catch over 500 coons with dogs" in the Great Smokies.

Raccoons are found throughout the Park at all elevations, although the Komareks stated that they are probably more common along the streams at lower altitudes. Localities where individuals have been seen include Laurel Creek, Greenbrier (2000 ft.), Hazel Creek at Proctor Creek, Walker Creek, Elkmont, Sugarlands (2400 ft.), Maddron Bald Trail, Walnut Bottoms, Round Bottom (3200 ft.), Alum Cave Bluffs, Mt. Sterling, and Mt. Le Conte (6300 ft.). Tracks have been found in several places throughout the Park. Traps set for the wild boar (*Sus scrofa*) have captured many blundering Raccoons. During the fall of 1962, 16 individuals were released from traps in the Twentymile area.

The breeding season for this species occurs in late January and early February, and the young are usually born around the beginning of April. Half-grown young were seen along the Appalachian Trail (5500 ft.) on October 3, 1940, and on the transmountain road in Tennessee (4400 ft.) on September 30, 1957.

The Raccoon is omnivorous, consuming both plant and animal foods. Beech mast is reputed to be a favorite item. Analyses of stomach contents and feces revealed that wild grapes, pokeberries, salamanders, and other aquatic animals were eaten in the Park (Komarek and Komarek, 1938). On two occasions, these mammals were reported to have killed many wood frogs (*Rana sylvatica*). It was also reported that a three-legged Raccoon entered a hen house in the Elkmont area and captured a chicken.

Illustration Number 23

Weasels, Skunks, and Other Mustelids
FAMILY MUSTELIDAE

This family is currently represented in the Park by four species. Although these forms are extremely diverse in appearance and habits, they have certain structural and biological characters in common. Usually they have long slender bodies, short legs, short rounded ears, and anal scent glands (Burt and Grossenheider, 1952). Members of this family are primarily nocturnal, although they may occasionally venture out during the daylight hours. All are active throughout the year except the Striped Skunk (*Mephitis mephitis*), which may sleep for several days at a time during the winter, although it is not considered a true hibernator. Habitat preferences vary widely among the members of this family and may change with the seasons.

Several species undergo an unusual reproductive process, which is known as delayed implantation. In this procedure, mating may occur in spring, summer, or fall. Shortly after fertilization, the embryo ceases to develop and does not attach, or implant, in the wall of the uterus for several months. Eventually, development resumes and the young are born after a gestation period that may be more than a year after mating has taken place. This type of reproduction is known to occur in the Fisher (*Martes pennanti*), River Otter (*Lutra canadensis*), and Long-tailed Weasel (*Mustela frenata*), but has not been reported in the Mink (*Mustela vison*), Striped Skunk (*Mephitis mephitis*), or Spotted Skunk (*Spilogale putorius*).

These animals are generally carnivorous and highly predaceous. The Fisher may attack animals larger than itself, and the fearless habits of weasels are well known. The Mink and River Otter often feed on aquatic animals, while skunks are omnivorous feeders. Most of the species have few natural enemies, although they are sought after by man for their pelts.

FISHER
Martes pennanti [Extirpated]

It is uncertain whether the Fisher ever occurred in the area encompassed by the Park. Miller and Kellogg (1955) noted that this animal was found as far south as North Carolina. This range was extended by Parmalee (1960), who found the jawbone of a Fisher in Bartow County, Georgia.

Audubon and Bachman (1846) stated: "We have seen several skins procured in east Tennessee. . . ." During a journey of several hundred miles through the mountains of Tennessee and North Carolina during the summer of 1887, Merriam (1888) found no trace of the Fisher, which he refers to as the "Pekan."

LONG-TAILED WEASEL
Mustela frenata

The Long-tailed Weasel is a fairly common resident of the Great Smoky Mountains National Park. This animal occurs at all altitudes, although the Komareks stated that it is probably not as common in the dense evergreen forests. Individuals have been observed along Little River (1400 ft.), Sugarlands (1500–1600 ft.), Noisy Creek, along the transmountain road (2900 ft., 4000 ft.), Greenbrier Pinnacle (4500 ft.), and Mt. Le Conte (6300 ft., 6593 ft.). Weasels are active throughout the year and, in northern areas, molt their brown summer fur and grow a new white coat. This white fur presumably acts as protective coloration, as well as radiating much less body heat than would a darker coat. Palmer (1954) stated that south of a line running from Virginia to Arizona, weasels retain their summer pelage all year. In the Park, no pelage change has ever been observed.

Long-tailed Weasels, which are slim mammals approximating gray squirrels in size, breed during July and August, and the young are born in April. In late April 1961, H. Brown discovered a nest of this species in a building near Le Conte Lodge. The nest contained 5 or 6 young, each about 4 inches in length with their eyes not yet open. (Palmer [1954] stated that the eyes open in 31 days.)

Although small rodents constitute the main food of weasels, they also feed upon birds, cold-blooded vertebrates, earthworms, and insects. In June 1944 an individual was seen on Mt. Le Conte carrying a deermouse (*Peromyscus* sp.) in its mouth.

Weasels have few natural enemies, a factor which may be attributed to their fearless and aggressive nature. In July 1953 a 16-inch Long-tailed Weasel was discovered in the stomach of a large timber rattlesnake (*Crotalus horridus*) taken near Caldwell Fork in the Cataloochee area. A few individuals have been found dead along Park roads.
Illustration Number 24

MINK
Mustela vison

Although relatively uncommon in the Park, the Mink is not rare. A former resident of the Sugarlands area recalls trapping two or three of these animals every winter. Mink, which are somewhat larger than weasels, are a uniform dark brown with a patch of white fur beneath the chin.

Mink occur at all altitudes in the Park. Komarek and Komarek (1938) reported that this species apparently frequents lower, more open situations in winter and retreats into the deeper forest to rear its young in spring and summer. Individuals have been seen near The Sinks (1500 ft.), at Big Creek, Metcalf Bottoms, Cades Cove, Sugarlands, Oconaluftee River, Greenbrier, Tremont, Cataloochee, Cliff Branch, Little River (1500 ft., 2900 ft.), Maddron Bald Trail, Mt. Sterling Creek (4000 ft.), Mt. Le Conte (6593 ft.).

Breeding occurs in February and March, and the young (usually five to eight) are born about six weeks later. On May 22, 1948, an individual estimated to be between six and eight weeks old was found near Cliff Branch. On June 15, 1935, an adult and six young were observed in the Cataloochee area (Fleetwood), while four young were discovered playing together along the Little River on July 15, 1959.

The food of the Mink includes fish, frogs, birds, and small mammals (Palmer, 1954). On one occasion, several individuals in the Cataloochee area were seen fighting over an 8-inch trout (Fleetwood).

Although the Mink spends much time in the water, a great deal of traveling is done on land, mainly at night (Palmer, 1954). In the 28 years that Stupka has been keeping records on the fauna of the Park, only four Mink were reported as having been found dead along Park roads.

Illustration Number 25

SPOTTED SKUNK
Spilogale putorius

The Spotted Skunk, or "civet," is a handsome member of the Park fauna, there being no other mammal with a similar color pattern. This skunk is black with a white spot on its forehead, one under each ear, and four broken white stripes along the neck, back, and sides. The tail has a white tip. The relative proportions of black and white vary considerably. The Komareks stated that this species was said to be less common than the Striped Skunk (*Mephitis mephitis*). In

1943, however, they were reported to be more plentiful in the Twentymile area of the Park.

The Spotted Skunk has been seen in the Park as high as 2800 ft. elevation, often occupying the same areas as the Striped Skunk. Individuals have been observed at Park Headquarters (1500 ft.), Sugarlands, Forney Creek, Greenbrier, Cataloochee, Big Creek (2800 ft.), and Walnut Bottoms.

Hamilton (1943) reported that this skunk is omnivorous, feeding upon such items as small mammals, fruits, insects, birds, lizards, snakes, and carrion. During January and February 1952 several individuals were liberated from garbage cans along the transmountain road in the Sugarlands area. The stomach of a specimen found near Park Headquarters in November 1950 contained the remains of a northern spring peeper (*Hyla crucifer*), a big short-tailed shrew (*Blarina brevicauda*), one katydid, one camel cricket, several clover leaves, and miscellaneous arthropod remains (Pfitzer).

Illustration Number 26

STRIPED SKUNK
Mephitis mephitis

This is the larger and more common of the two skunks inhabiting the Great Smoky Mountains National Park. It may be recognized by its black body, narrow white stripe up the middle of its forehead, and broad white area on its neck that usually divides into a V approximately at the shoulders. It has been observed at elevations up to 5200 ft. Specimens have been recorded in many localities including Cades Cove (1800 ft.), Sugarlands (2000 ft.), Elkmont (2000 ft.), Greenbrier (3000 ft.), Walnut Bottoms, Mingus and Cooper Creek Divide (3500 ft.), Spence Field (5000 ft.), Newfound Gap, and Indian Gap (5200 ft.). Komarek and Komarek (1938) remarked that the Striped Skunk is generally distributed throughout the mountains but is probably more commonly associated with the open fields and cut-over woodlands of the lower elevations.

Although skunks are known to sleep for prolonged periods during cold weather (not hibernation), active individuals have been observed in the Park during every month of the year.

Palmer (1954) reported that the food of the Striped Skunk consists mainly of small rodents, cold-blooded vertebrates, insects, and some vegetable matter. In February 1935 a skunk was observed on Messer Fork following a plow and eating grubs (Fleetwood). On November 26, 1937, Stupka examined the stomach of an individual found near Elkmont and noted the seeds and pulp of persimmon, insect remains (grasshopper, Hemiptera, and larvae) and the feathers of a small bird.

Because of its well-known and effective defense mechanism, the Striped Skunk is not molested by many animals. Palmer (1954) stated, however, that "practically every Horned Owl in the skunk's range smells of skunk—one of its staple foods." On two occasions in the Park, Stupka noted great horned owls (*Bubo virginianus*) which had a strong odor of skunk about them.

Illustration Number 27

RIVER OTTER
Lutra canadensis [Extirpated]

Otters are large weasel-like mammals with a broad rounded snout, webbed feet, and a stout tapering tail. According to Rhoads (1896), the River Otter was "a rare but constant inhabitant of all the larger streams in the State [Tennessee]." Buckley (1859) reported that otter skins were among those bought by traveling fur merchants in the Smokies. However, due to uncontrolled trapping by man, this species has been exterminated in many areas, including the Great Smoky Mountains National Park.

Otters, or "orters" as they were known to the mountain hunters, have been recorded at Sugarlands, Big Creek, Greenbrier, Bryson Place, Cataloochee, Gregory Bald, and Mt. Sterling. This species was last seen in the Park in 1927, when three individuals were sighted in the Cataloochee area. Willis King stated in 1937, however, that otters "occurred in the Smokies less than 10 years ago."

The reintroduction of the River Otter in the Park was given serious consideration, but because otters are known to travel long distances, it was believed they would emigrate from the area.

Illustration Number 28

Cats
FAMILY FELIDAE

This familiar family is generally characterized by the short face, relatively small rounded ears, and retractile claws of its members (Burt and Grossenheider, 1952). Formerly, two native members of this group inhabited the Park—the Bobcat (*Lynx rufus*) and the Mountain Lion or Cougar (*Felis concolor*). The latter species is now generally believed to be extinct in this area. Although some think the Lynx (*Lynx canadensis*) was once here, its presence in the Park has never been verified.

Where members of this family occur, they prefer to live in remote regions, although the Bobcat is fairly tolerant of man's presence. The cats are variable in their activity patterns. Some, like the Mountain Lion, may be abroad both day and night, whereas others, exemplified by the Bobcat, are nocturnal creatures. All species are active throughout the seasons.

The members of this family are carnivorous and feed upon mammals, birds, reptiles, and a variety of other animals. Other than man, there are few natural enemies.

MOUNTAIN LION
Felis concolor [Extirpated]

The largest member of the cat family known to have occurred in the Great Smoky Mountains National Park, the Mountain Lion may also be known as "cougar," "catamount," and "puma." The present status of the "panther" or "painter," as this large, long-tailed cat is sometimes called in the Southern Appalachian region, is uncertain. Palmer (1954) stated: "There is reason to believe that it exists in small numbers in some areas where it has long been thought to be absent. . . ." The Park files contain a number of reports of persons who believe they have seen a Mountain Lion.

The first record of this species in the Park dates back to 1840–1850 when John Oliver reported that he heard of two "panthers" being killed in Cades Cove. In 1859, Buckley noted that the "panther" was troublesome to the mountain farmers of North Carolina and Tennessee, destroying their sheep and hogs.

Brimley (1944), writing about the mammals of North Carolina, recorded the Mountain Lion as being "apparently extinct," the last specimens having been killed near Highlands and in Craven County about 1886. After a journey through the Great Smoky Mountains during the summer of 1887, Merriam (1888) reported that the panther was "unknown."

Between 1895 and 1905, a panther was reported by William Barnes on Big Creek. There are reports of two panthers being killed about 1899—one near Smokemont and the other in the Greenbrier area of the Park.

During the early winter of 1920, Tom Sparks was said to have been attacked by a panther while herding sheep on Spence Field (Brewer, 1964). He managed to inflict a deep wound in its left shoulder. Several months later, W. Orr killed a panther near what is now Fontana Village and found that its left shoulder blade was cut in two. This was generally believed to be the same cat that Mr. Sparks had wounded. This is reputed to be the last panther killed in the Great Smokies. In 1928, Ganier reported that the panther was extinct in Tennessee, "save possibly a half dozen individuals in the Great Smokies."

Hamnett and Thornton (1953), in discussing the status of this cat, stated that it is "now believed to be extinct. . . . Last positive records for the State were from the Coastal Region . . . in the early 1900's. . . . Until positive proof of the cougar's existence is furnished . . . we must continue to regard this animal as virtually extinct in North Carolina."

Many additional reports of persons who believe they have seen a Mountain Lion are contained in Park files. None of these reports, however, has been verified by a qualified observer, nor have any photographs, footprint casts, and the like ever been presented as supporting evidence. The following data on supposed Mountain Lion sightings is given only for the purpose of providing a complete account of reported occurrences of this species in the Park.

> 1938–Black Camp Gap near Bunches Creek
> Appalachian Trail near Newfound Gap
> Near School House Gap

1939–Gregory Bald—Parson Bald area

1940–Tremont

Chimneys Campground

1957–Pauls Gap

1958–Fighting Creek Gap

1959–Smokemont

1967–Near Newfound Gap

Although many of these reports are quite interesting and provide descriptions of an animal resembling a Mountain Lion, they are not sufficient to establish its presence. Until definite evidence of this species' presence in this area can be obtained, the Mountain Lion must be considered extirpated from the Park.

Illustration Number 29

BOBCAT
Lynx rufus

The Bobcat, or Wildcat, is a fairly common resident of the Park. Its smaller size and short tail readily distinguish this species from the Mountain Lion (*Felis concolor*).

Komarek and Komarek (1938) concluded that the Bobcat was generally distributed throughout the mountains at all elevations. Individuals have been recorded from Cades Cove, Greenbrier, Little River Road, Couches Creek, Cliff Branch (2600 ft.), Newt Prong at the head of Jakes Creek, Mt. Le Conte (6593 ft.), and Clingmans Dome. Bobcat tracks and droppings have been reported from several additional localities.

Young (1958) noted that adult Bobcats usually weigh between 18 and 25 pounds, although males weighing 30 to 35 pounds are not uncommon. Two adult specimens obtained from Tapoco, North Carolina (near the Park boundary), weighed 17 and 20 pounds, respectively (Alcoa News, 1941).

Young (1958), discussing the reproductive habits of this species, said that breeding occurs throughout the year, but mainly in late winter, with an average of two kits being born after a gestation period of 50 to 60 days. Yearlings usually weigh between 8 and 12 pounds (Palmer, 1954). On February 9, 1959, a yearling weighing

5 pounds, 1 ounce, was found dead along the Little River road (Stupka, 1959).

The Bobcat is carnivorous, feeding upon a variety of small animals as well as occasional large mammals, such as deer (Marston, 1942). Young (1958) stated that in the South, the opossum (*Didelphis marsupialis*) is a favored food. Hamilton (1943) remarked: "A few stomachs which I examined from the Smoky Mountains of North Carolina contained the remains of beetles, rabbits and a small box turtle." A specimen discovered near the Park boundary in Wears Cove in March 1941 had the remains of a robin in its stomach (Stupka, 1941). In August 1952, Stupka examined an adult Bobcat that had been killed by a car on the transmountain road in Tennessee (3700 ft.). A stomach analysis revealed the following food items: 8 shrews (*Sorex* sp.), 6 woodland jumping mice (*Napaeozapus insignis*), 5 yellow-nosed voles (*Microtus chrotorrhinus*), 1 deermouse (*Peromyscus* sp.), and 1 small bird. Examination of an individual found dead near Cliff Branch (2600 ft.) in December 1953 revealed that it had eaten a gray squirrel (*Sciurus carolinensis*) (Stupka, 1953).

Palmer (1954) noted that "usually a kill is at least partly covered with debris, and the Bobcat returns to feed again." On January 18, 1938, a freshly killed, partially eaten woodchuck (*Marmota monax*) covered with leaves was found by Stupka above Big Cove (3200 ft.) near the Park boundary. Many Bobcat tracks were present in the snow nearby. Adult Bobcats have few enemies, although young animals fall prey at times to foxes and horned owls (Young, 1958).

Illustration Number 30

Pigs

FAMILY SUIDAE

The members of this family belong to the even-toed hoofed animals and are native to the Old World. They include the domestic pig or hog and the wild boar, the latter having been introduced into various areas of the United States for game purposes. The European Wild Boar is the only member of this family inhabiting the Park.

Boars can be distinguished from domestic pigs by several features. The head is long, ending in a slender, mobile snout. The bristles of the boar split at the end into from one to five prongs with the tips silvery in color, and the ears are small, pointed, and very hairy. Wild boars also have narrower hooves and longer legs than domestic swine, and the tail is long and mule-like, with a large tuft of long hair at the tip. The canine teeth of the European Wild Boar are well developed in both sexes and, in the males, these become large, upwardly directed tusks.

EUROPEAN WILD BOAR
Sus scrofa

The European Wild Boar is a non-native member of the fauna of the Great Smoky Mountains National Park. Because this pig is not native to the Park and because of its destructive habits, efforts are being made to eliminate this species from the Park, where it occurs commonly in the western section. On some of the grassy balds, one can observe large areas of bare soil where the sod has been uprooted by these animals in their search for food.

The European Wild Boar is described by Stegeman (1938) as attaining a height of over 3 feet at the shoulder and a weight of over 400 pounds. The body is built somewhat like that of a buffalo, being higher and heavier in the shoulder region.

It is not known how or when the European Wild Boar came to the Park. Thirteen young boars, weighing 60 to 75 pounds apiece, first arrived in Murphy, North Carolina (approximately 40 miles south of the Park), in April 1912, destined for a game preserve on Hooper Bald, where they were released. It is believed that the animals had been purchased through an agent in Berlin, who said they came from Russia. In any case, the boars dispersed from the preserve and made their way into the Great Smoky Mountains National Park.

Boar depredations were first noted on the state line in 1958. In 1959 it was found that these animals were concentrated in the area between Cades Cove and Fontana Lake. Trapping began during August 1959, at which time there were an estimated 500 boars in the Park. As of March 1, 1969, a total of 315 of these animals had been trapped. The largest boar that has been captured in the Park was a male weighing 303 pounds; it was taken on Welch Branch in September 1962.

Little is known of the life history and habits of the European Wild Boar in the United States. The original stock has hybridized freely with feral domestic pigs. Stegeman (1938) concluded that in Tennessee this animal has two breeding seasons, one in December or January, and another in April or May. Although the number of litters per year is unknown, there is some indication that there may be two. It has been reported that the litter size ranges from three to eight, but four or five are the most common numbers (Jones, 1957). An individual accompanied by two young was seen near Cades Cove during September 1962. It is also known that at the age of one year, the permanent tusks begin to grow, and at one and one-half years, the European Wild Boar reaches sexual maturity (Stegeman, 1938). Stegeman (1938) also noted that the longitudinal stripes marking the young animal at birth disappear within six months.

Wild boars are known to be omnivorous, feeding on plant matter and invertebrate and small vertebrate life (Stegeman, 1938). Hamnett and Thornton (1953) indicated that these mammals are "dependent on a sufficient supply of mast" for food.

Due to its large size, the European Wild Boar has relatively few predators. The bobcat (*Lynx rufus*) is one of the boar's worst enemies, damage probably being limited to the young pigs. Both young and adult wild boars are preyed upon by the black bear (*Ursus americanus*) (Stegeman, 1938).

Illustration Number 31

Deer

FAMILY CERVIDAE

This family includes hoofed mammals having antlers that are shed each year (Burt and Grossenheider, 1952). Two members of this group have been known to inhabit the Park, although at present the American Elk (*Cervus canadensis*) has been extirpated and only the White-tailed Deer (*Odocoileus virginianus*) still occurs.

Deer are herbivorous and graze or browse on a variety of plants, shrubs, and trees. The American Elk is less selective in its diet than is the White-tailed Deer (Palmer, 1954). During the winter, some species, like the elk, may migrate to wintering grounds at lower elevations, whereas others, such as the White-tailed Deer, "yard-up" in restricted areas.

Breeding in this group occurs in the latter part of the year. The species are polygamous, and a male may collect a harem of several females. Violent battles often occur between males during the breeding or "rutting" season. The antlers, a characteristic of this family, play a role in these fights. These structures, composed of true bone, are shed from late fall to early spring.

AMERICAN ELK (WAPITI)
Cervus canadensis [Extirpated]

At one time the American Elk roamed throughout the Southern Appalachian Mountains, but it has since been extirpated. In 1896, Rhoads stated: "At the beginning of the present century, this noble animal was probably a visitant to every county in the State [Tennessee]." Ganier (1928) reported that the last one in eastern Tennessee was shot in 1849.

In discussing the status of this mammal in North Carolina, Hamnett and Thornton (1953) reported that it "once inhabited at least a portion of North Carolina including the northern Piedmont and Mountain counties. It is doubtful if they were ever very numerous, however, since this region was near the southern limits of their range." They stated further that "it probably was present in the Mountain Region until the late 1700's." Brimley (1945) recorded that elk occurred in colonial times in the mountains (North Carolina) at least until 1750. Cope (1870) noted that horns of elk were found in the Black Mountains in western North Carolina in the early 1800's.

WHITE-TAILED DEER
Odocoileus virginianus

One of our largest mammals, White-tailed Deer were once common in some sections of the area now included in the Park. However, due to a combination of factors—persistent hunting, running by dogs, disease, and predators—they decreased in numbers, almost disappearing from the Park by about 1930. The formation of the Park at that period provided a refuge for these animals, and they have been increasing ever since. Deer remained scarce until the late 1940's, when small herds of seven or eight animals were reported in Cades Cove. By the middle 1950's, the herd in Cades Cove had built up considerably and, since that time, they have frequently been observed there. By the early 1960's, White-tailed Deer were being reported from many places in the Park. At the present time, they are fairly common, especially in the western third of the Park. They are scarce or absent in the spruce-fir region. Other than Cades Cove, deer have been reported from Fontana Lake, Hazel Creek, Noland Creek, Deep Creek, Collins Creek, Big Creek, Cosby, Greenbrier, near Fighting Creek, Heintooga, Cataloochee, and Smokemont.

White-tailed Deer inhabit mixed or deciduous woodland having an understory as well as forest edges, usually not far from water. They avoid dense stands of mature conifers (except in winter) and very extensive open areas (Palmer, 1954).

In this area, deer usually breed during the latter months of the year. On November 1, 1956, mating deer were observed in Cades Cove (Stupka, 1956). The young are born after a gestation period of approximately 196 days. Usually there is one fawn in the first litter, with two being common thereafter (Taylor, 1956). A doe and a newly born fawn were observed on June 20, 1956, in Cades Cove (Stupka, 1956). The tracks of an adult and fawn were seen along the Gregory Ridge Trail (4200 ft.) on June 17, 1939 (Stupka, 1939), and several does with fawns were noted near Hazel Creek in August 1963.

Deer are active at all hours, although much less so during the day. They usually commence feeding with the approach of dusk and continue to move about during the night, usually bedding down with the approach of dawn (Hamilton, 1943).

Due to their large size, White-tailed Deer have relatively few enemies. Among the worst of these are dogs that come into the Park from surrounding areas, chase the deer until they are near exhaustion, and subsequently kill them. Other predators include the black bear (*Ursus americanus*), bobcat (*Lynx rufus*), and the European wild boar (*Sus scrofa*). Persistent hunting in the vicinity of the Park has also taken its toll.

The Komareks (1938) referred to a disease among the deer population as a possible decimating factor. Hamnett and Thornton (1953) noted that "disease has been an important factor affecting deer numbers in North Carolina. . . ." This disease was probably hemorrhagic septicemia, commonly known as "black tongue." It causes the rupture of small blood vessels under the skin and in the liver and other organs.

Illustration Number 32 and front cover

Bison

FAMILY BOVIDAE

This family of even-toed hoofed animals includes our domestic cattle, sheep, and goats. Members are characterized by having unbranched horns that are never shed. Horns are present on both sexes in all but a few forms. Although no members of this family occur in the Park at present, the Bison, or buffalo, once inhabited the area.

BISON
Bison bison [Extirpated]

Bison were probably extirpated in this part of the country during the late eighteenth century. Brimley (1945) recorded that these mammals originally ranged over much of North Carolina but were exterminated about 1760.

Dr. J. A. Allen (1876) summarized information regarding the history of this animal in Tennessee. He noted that they formerly passed over the Cumberland and Great Smoky mountain ranges by way of the Holston and French Broad rivers, to and from the Great Valley of East Tennessee. However, the majority were confined to the Cumberland Valley and its tributaries. He concluded that the point of greatest abundance was undoubtedly in the blue-grass region of the vicinity of Nashville and reported that the "hills and coves of the Allegheny Mountains in Tennessee," which were covered with large tracts of native grasses, attracted the Bison from the lowlands in the summer.

Kellogg (1939) noted that the number of Bison in eastern Tennessee was never very great, but that they were "present in some numbers" in the western part of the state. He quoted Ramsey (1853), who stated that in 1783, a locality in Cumberland County was a "vast upland prairie, covered with a most luxuriant growth of native grasses, pastured over as far as the eye could see, with numerous herds of deer, elk and buffalo." Apparently, some Bison were still present in the region around Nashville in June 1795 and in Putnam County in December 1799. In 1823, Haywood stated that "at this time there is not one in the whole State of Tennessee."

Mammals
of Surrounding Areas

The following nine species are known to occur in regions surrounding the Great Smoky Mountains National Park. Some of these species may be recorded in the Park in the future.

SOUTHEASTERN MYOTIS
Myotis austroriparius

Although never recorded from the Great Smoky Mountains National Park, this bat species has been found both north and south of the area (Hall and Kelson, 1959).

GRAY MYOTIS
Myotis grisescens

Hamilton (1943) listed this species as occurring in all of Tennessee and into western North Carolina. The northeasternmost locality given by Hall and Kelson (1959) was Indian Cave, Grainger County, Tennessee, which is north of the Park. Smith, Funderburg, and Quay (1960) reported that this bat probably occurs in the southwestern mountains of North Carolina. More recently, Holsinger (1964) located a large colony in Grigsby Cave, a few miles southeast of Nickelsville, Scott County, Virginia. This locality is 13 miles north of the Tennessee-Virginia line.

LEAST MYOTIS
Myotis subulatus

This species has been taken in areas surrounding the Park.* Adams (1950) recorded specimens from Bat Cave, Henderson County, North Carolina, about 50 miles east of the Park. Two additional individuals were noted on January 19, 1934, at Talc Mountain, 14 miles northeast of Andrews, Swain County, North Carolina (Schwartz, 1954). Recently, Tuttle (1964b) found individuals near Dayton, Rhea County, Tennessee, approximately 65 miles west of the Great Smoky Mountains National Park.

---

* Since this manuscript went into production, a specimen of the Least Myotis was found in the Park. The individual, an adult female, was collected by Hans Neuhauser in the Great Smoky Mountains Hiking Club Cabin, Porters Flat, Sevier County, Tennessee, on April 24, 1970. The elevation was approximately 2200 ft. (personal communication from H. Neuhauser, May 11, 1970).

HOARY BAT
Lasiurus cinereus

The Hoary Bat ranges over the entire United States with the exception of southern Florida (Hall and Kelson, 1959). Smith, Funderburg, and Quay (1960) listed it as statewide but uncommon in North Carolina. Kellogg (1939) recorded no specimens from the state of Tennessee.

EVENING BAT
Nycticeius humeralis

According to Hall and Kelson (1959), this bat ranges over the entire southeastern United States. It has been called the "third commonest species" in North Carolina (Brimley, 1944–1946). Paul and Quay (1963) reported one individual from the Toxaway River Gorge. Kellogg (1939) recorded specimens from counties in Tennessee west of the mountains.

WESTERN LUMP-NOSED BAT
Corynorhinus townsendii

The Park is well within the range of this bat (Hall and Kelson, 1959). However, Kellogg (1939) and Smith, Funderburg, and Quay (1960) reported no specimens from Tennessee and North Carolina, respectively.

PORCUPINE
Erethizon dorsatum

The nearest records of this species are in West Virginia, although Hall and Kelson (1959) indicated that its range may extend through the mountains as far south as the Smokies. Jawbones of Porcupines have been recovered from archeological sites west of Chattanooga in Marion County, Tennessee (Parmalee and Guilday, 1966).

COYOTE
Canis latrans

A symbol of the western prairies, the Coyote has been rapidly extending its range eastward. Hamilton (1943) reported this species as occurring sporadically in nearly every eastern state. Young and Jackson (1951) noted that within the past two decades Coyotes made their first appearance in Tennessee and North Carolina. In the Southern states particularly, Hamilton noted that many have been liberated by fox hunters who have received shipments of Coyote pups instead of young foxes, to which as pups they bear a striking resemblance. Brimley (1944) noted that there had been rumors in recent years of Coyotes having been released in the mountains, but no positive evidence had been found. A forest ranger on the Cherokee Indian Reservation in Swain County, North Carolina, reported the positive identification of one animal killed in 1947 (Hamnett and Thornton, 1953). Smith, Funderburg, and Quay (1960) noted that Coyotes have been recorded from all of the states bordering North Carolina, and that they possibly occur in the mountains in small numbers.

LEAST WEASEL
Mustela nivalis

This weasel has been taken in western North Carolina on four occasions. On April 17, 1916, the first specimen was reported from Marshall, Madison County, approximately 25 miles northeast of the Park (Church, 1925). The second weasel was taken from a cat at Balsam Gap (3400 ft.), Jackson County, on July 24, 1959 (Stupka, 1960a). This locality is approximately 10 miles southeast of the Park. Edwards (1963) took a third individual near Asheville, 25 miles east of the Park. A fourth North Carolina specimen was recorded on November 17, 1965, 4 miles northeast of Hendersonville, Henderson County, at an altitude of 2200 ft. (Barkalow, 1967). This locality is within 10 miles of the South Carolina border and represents the southernmost limit of the species. The lone Tennessee record of the Least Weasel is a specimen taken on Roan Mountain (4800 ft.), Carter County, on September 25, 1962 (Tuttle, 1968). This locality is approximately 70 miles northeast of the Great Smoky Mountains National Park.

Appendixes

Checklist of Mammals

Great Smoky Mountains National Park

All scientific names are those of Miller and Kellogg (1955), unless changes have been made subsequent to the publication of their list, in which case the paper proposing the name change is given in the list of literature cited. Extirpated species are marked with an asterisk.

FAMILY DIDELPHIDAE
  Didelphis marsupialis virginiana Kerr   Opossum

FAMILY SORICIDAE
  Sorex cinereus cinereus Kerr   Common Shrew
  Sorex fumeus fumeus Miller   Smoky Shrew
  Sorex longirostris longirostris Bachman   Southeastern Shrew
  Sorex dispar blitchi Schwartz (Schwartz, 1956)   Long-tailed Shrew
  Sorex palustris punctulatus Hooper   Northern Water Shrew
  Microsorex hoyi winnemana Preble   Pigmy Shrew
  Blarina brevicauda churchi Bole and Moulthrop   Big Short-tailed Shrew
  Cryptotis parva parva (Say)   Little Short-tailed Shrew

FAMILY TALPIDAE
  Parascalops breweri (Bachman)   Hairy-tailed Mole
  Scalopus aquaticus aquaticus (Linnaeus)   Eastern Mole
  Condylura cristata parva Paradiso (Paradiso, 1959)   Star-nosed Mole

FAMILY VESPERTILIONIDAE
  Myotis lucifugus lucifugus (Le Conte)   Little Brown Myotis
  Myotis keenii septentrionalis (Trouessart)   Keen's Myotis
  Myotis sodalis Miller and G. M. Allen   Indiana Bat
  Lasionycteris noctivagans (Le Conte)   Silver-haired Bat
  Pipistrellus subflavus subflavus (F. Cuvier)   Eastern Pipistrelle
  Eptesicus fuscus fuscus (Beauvois)   Big Brown Bat
  Lasiurus borealis borealis (Müller)   Red Bat
  Corynorhinus rafinesquii (Lesson)   Eastern Lump-nosed Bat

FAMILY LEPORIDAE
  Sylvilagus floridanus mallurus (Thomas)   Eastern Cottontail
  Sylvilagus transitionalis (Bangs)   New England Cottontail

FAMILY SCIURIDAE
  Marmota monax monax (Linnaeus)   Woodchuck
  Tamias striatus striatus (Linnaeus)   Eastern Chipmunk

Sciurus carolinensis   Eastern Gray Squirrel
Intergrade between *Sciurus c. carolinensis* Gmelin and *Sciurus carolinensis pennsylvanicus* Ord (Barbour, 1951)
Sciurus niger niger Linnaeus   Eastern Fox Squirrel
Tamiasciurus hudsonicus abieticola (A. H. Howell)   Red Squirrel
Glaucomys volans   Southern Flying Squirrel
Intergrade between *Glaucomys v. volans* (Linnaeus) and *Glaucomys volans saturatus* A. H. Howell (Barbour, 1951)
Glaucomys sabrinus coloratus Handley   Northern Flying Squirrel

FAMILY CASTORIDAE
    Castor canadensis carolinensis Rhoads   Beaver

FAMILY CRICETIDAE
    Oryzomys palustris palustris (Harlan)   Rice Rat
    Reithrodontomys humulis humulis (Audubon and Bachman)   Eastern Harvest Mouse
    Peromyscus leucopus   Woodland Deermouse
        Intergrade between *Peromyscus l. leucopus* (Rafinesque) and *Peromyscus leucopus noveboracensis* (Fischer) (Barbour, 1951)
    Peromyscus maniculatus nubiterrae Rhoads   Long-tailed Deermouse
    Peromyscus gossypinus megacephalus (Rhoads)   Cotton Deermouse
    Ochrotomys nuttalli nuttalli (Harlan)   Golden Deermouse
        This species was removed from *Peromyscus* by Hooper (1958).
    Sigmodon hispidus komareki Gardner   Common Cotton Rat
    Neotoma floridana haematoreia (A. H. Howell)   Eastern Woodrat
    Synaptomys cooperi stonei Rhoads   Southern Lemming Mouse
    Clethrionomys gapperi carolinensis (Merriam)   Northern Red-backed Mouse
    Microtus pennsylvanicus pennsylvanicus (Ord)   Meadow Vole
    Microtus chrotorrhinus carolinensis Komarek   Yellow-nosed Vole
    Microtus pinetorum   Pine Mouse
        This species was placed in the genus *Microtus* by Hall and Cockrum (1953). The ranges of three subspecies (*carbonarius, pinetorum,* and *scalopsoides*) meet in the Park area. The identity of Park specimens has not been determined.
    Ondatra zibethicus zibethicus (Linnaeus)   Muskrat

FAMILY MURIDAE
    Rattus norvegicus norvegicus (Berkenhout)   Brown Rat
    Rattus rattus rattus (Linnaeus)   Black Rat
    Mus musculus brevirostris Waterhouse   House Mouse

FAMILY ZAPODIDAE
    Zapus hudsonius americanus (Barton)   Northern Meadow Jumping Mouse
    Napaeozapus insignis roanensis (Preble)   Woodland Jumping Mouse

FAMILY CANIDAE
    Canis lupus lycaon (Schreber)   Gray Wolf
    Vulpes fulva fulva (Desmarest)   Red Fox

Urocyon cinereoargenteus cinereoargenteus (Schreber)   Gray Fox

FAMILY URSIDAE
Ursus americanus americanus Pallas   Black Bear

FAMILY PROCYONIDAE
Procyon lotor varius Nelson and Goldman   Raccoon

FAMILY MUSTELIDAE
*Martes pennanti pennanti (Erxleben)   Fisher
Mustela frenata noveboracensis (Emmons)   Long-tailed Weasel
Mustela vison mink Peale and Beauvois   Mink
Spilogale putorius (Linnaeus)   Spotted Skunk
Mephitis mephitis elongata Bangs   Striped Skunk
*Lutra canadensis canadensis (Schreber)   River Otter

FAMILY FELIDAE
*Felis concolor couguar Kerr   Mountain Lion
Lynx rufus rufus (Schreber)   Bobcat

FAMILY SUIDAE
Sus scrofa   European Wild Boar

FAMILY CERVIDAE
*Cervus canadensis canadensis Erxleben   American Elk (Wapiti)
Odocoileus virginianus virginianus (Zimmermann)   White-tailed Deer

FAMILY BOVIDAE
*Bison bison bison (Linnaeus)   Bison

Localities
Referred to in Text

ABRAMS CREEK   857–3075 ft.
Near western boundary of Park (Tenn.)

ABRAMS CREEK RANGER STATION   1200 ft.
Western boundary of Park (Tenn.)

ALUM CAVE BLUFFS   4900 ft.
South slope of Mt. Le Conte (Tenn.)

ALUM CAVE PARKING AREA   3800 ft.
Along transmountain road (Tenn.)

ALUM CAVE TRAIL   3800–6300 ft.
South slope of Mt. Le Conte (Tenn.)

ANDREWS BALD   5800 ft.
South of Clingmans Dome (N. C.)

APPALACHIAN TRAIL   mostly 5000–6000 ft.
Approximately along Tenn.–N. C. line

BECKS BALD   5022 ft.
Near southeastern boundary, west of Hughes Ridge (N. C.)

BIG COVE   2500 ft.
Cherokee Indian Reservation, east of Smokemont (N. C.)

BIG CREEK   approx. 1500–4900 ft.
Near northeastern boundary of Park (N. C.)

BLACK CAMP GAP   4522 ft.
Near southeastern boundary of Park (N. C.)

BLANKET MOUNTAIN   4609 ft. (summit)
Southwest of Elkmont (Tenn.)

BOTE MOUNTAIN   approx. 4800 ft. (summit)
East of Cades Cove (Tenn.)

BOULEVARD TRAIL   6000–6593 ft.
Mt. Kephart (Tenn.–N. C.) to Mt. Le Conte (Tenn.)

BRADLEY FORK   approx. 2200–3000 ft.
Tributary of Oconaluftee River north of Smokemont (N. C.)

BRYSON PLACE   2411 ft.
Along Deep Creek, north of Bryson City (N. C.)

BUCK FORK   approx. 2950–5350 ft.
Greenbrier area, branch of Middle Prong of Little Pigeon River (Tenn.)

BUCKHORN AREA   1500 ft.
North of Park boundary, east of Gatlinburg (Tenn.)

BULL CAVE   1900 ft.
Northern boundary of Park, near Rich Mountain (Tenn.)

BUNCHES CREEK   approx. 2400–4400 ft.
Flows along southeastern boundary of Park near Black Camp Gap (N. C.)

CADES COVE   mostly 1800–1900 ft.
Western part of Park (Tenn.)

CATALOOCHEE   approx. 2600 ft.
Cove near eastern boundary of Park (N. C.)

CHAMBERS CREEK   approx. 1700 ft. (mouth)
Tributary of the Tuckaseegee River, west of Bryson City (N. C.)

CHAPMAN PRONG   approx. 3450–5150 ft.
Tributary of Ramsey Prong, in Greenbrier section (Tenn.)

CHARLIES BUNION   5375 ft.
On Appalachian Trail, northeast of Newfound Gap (Tenn.–N. C.)

CHEROKEE   approx. 1900 ft.
Town on Cherokee Indian Reservation adjacent to southern boundary of Park (N. C.)

CHEROKEE ORCHARD   2600 ft.
Four miles southeast of Gatlinburg (Tenn.)

CHILHOWEE MOUNTAINS   approx. 1500–2700 ft.
Outside Park, just beyond northwestern boundary (Tenn.)

CHIMNEYS CAMPGROUND   2700 ft.
Along transmountain road, 6 miles south of Gatlinburg (Tenn.)

CLIFF BRANCH   approx. 2600–3800 ft.
Tributary of Oconaluftee River, north of Thomas Divide (N. C.)

CLINGMANS DOME   6643 ft. (summit)
Along state line at head of Forney Ridge, highest point in Park (Tenn.–N. C.)

CLINGMANS DOME ROAD   5040–6311 ft.
From Newfound Gap to Clingmans Dome Parking Area (N. C.)

COLLINS CREEK   approx. 2400–4550 ft.
Tributary of the Oconaluftee River above Smokemont (N. C.)

COLLINS GAP   5720 ft.
Between Indian Gap and Clingmans Dome (Tenn.–N. C.)

COOPER CREEK   approx. 1900–4640 ft.
Along southern boundary of Park near Thomas Divide (N. C.)

COSBY   approx. 1400 ft.
Town north of Park boundary near northeast corner of Park (Tenn.)

COSBY CAMPGROUND   approx. 2400 ft.
Northeast corner of Park (Tenn.)

COSBY CREEK   approx. 1650–4200 ft.
Near northeastern boundary of Park (Tenn.)

COSBY RANGER STATION   1750 ft.
Near northeastern boundary of Park (Tenn.)

COUCHES CREEK   approx. 2050–3700 ft.
Tributary of Oconaluftee River near Smokemont (N. C.)

DEEP CREEK   approx. 1792–4000 ft.
North of Bryson City (N. C.)

DEEP CREEK RANGER STATION   1900 ft.
North of Bryson City (N. C.)

DRY SLUICE GAP   5375 ft.
Between Charlies Bunion and the Sawteeth on state line, east of Newfound Gap (Tenn.–N. C.)

DRY VALLEY   1200–1500 ft.
Town between northern boundary of Park and Townsend (Tenn.)

DUDLEY CREEK   approx. 1400–3500 ft.
Flows along northern Park boundary, east of Gatlinburg (Tenn.)

EAGLE CREEK   approx. 1700–2500 ft.
North of Fontana Lake (N. C.)

EAGLE ROCKS CREEK   approx. 3250–4950 ft.
Tributary of Middle Prong of Little Pigeon River in Greenbrier area (Tenn.)

ELKMONT   2146 ft.
On Little River, southwest of Park Headquarters (Tenn.)

FIGHTING CREEK   approx. 1442–3250 ft.
Tributary of the West Prong of the Little Pigeon River (Tenn.)

FIGHTING CREEK GAP   2320 ft.
On Little River Road, 4 miles west of Park Headquarters (Tenn.)

FISH CAMP PRONG   approx. 2750–4650 ft.
Tributary of Little River, southeast of Elkmont (Tenn.)

FLAT CREEK   approx. 4000–5000 ft.
South of Heintooga Overlook, near southeastern boundary of Park (N. C.)

FONTANA DAM   approx. 1700 ft.
Near southwestern boundary of Park (N. C.)

FONTANA LAKE   between 1700–1800 ft.
Along southwestern boundary of Park (N. C.)

FONTANA VILLAGE   approx. 2000 ft.
Near southwestern boundary of Park (N. C.)

FORNEY CREEK   approx. 1600–5700 ft.
Flows southwest from vicinity of Clingmans Dome to Fontana Reservoir
(N. C.)

FORT HARRY CLIFFS   3200 ft.
Rock cliffs above Buckeye Nature Trail (Tenn.)

GATLINBURG   1293 ft.
Town on north-central boundary of Park (Tenn.)

GNATTY BRANCH   approx. 1100 ft.
Tributary of West Prong of Little Pigeon River; flows along Foothills
Parkway between Gatlinburg and Pigeon Forge (Tenn.)

GRASSY PATCH   (see Alum Cave Parking Area)

GREENBRIER   1680 ft.
Approximately 10 miles east of Gatlinburg (Tenn.)

GREENBRIER PINNACLE   4805 ft. (summit)
East of Greenbrier, near northeastern boundary of Park (Tenn.)

GREGORY BALD   4948 ft.
On state-line ridge, southwest of Cades Cove (Tenn.–N. C.)

GREGORY RIDGE TRAIL   1930–4600 ft.
From near Cades Cove to state-line ridge (Tenn.)

GUM STAND   approx. 1100 ft.
Outside Park boundary between Gatlinburg and Pigeon Forge (Tenn.)

HAPPY VALLEY   1332 ft.
On western boundary of Park near Chilhowee Mt. (Tenn.)

HAZEL CREEK   approx. 2100–5150 ft.
Flows into Fontana Reservoir between Eagle Creek and Forney Creek
(N. C.)

HEINTOOGA OVERLOOK   5325 ft.
Terminus of Blue Ridge Parkway spur that leaves Parkway at Mile 458.2; vicinity of southeastern boundary of Park (N. C.)

INADU KNOB   5941 ft.
On state-line ridge, north of Mt. Guyot; in northeastern part of Park (Tenn.–N. C.)

INDIAN CAMP CREEK   approx. 1850–4850 ft.
North of Old Black Mountain in northeastern section of Park (Tenn.)

INDIAN CREEK   approx. 1900–4350 ft.
Tributary of Deep Creek near boundary of Park, north of Bryson City (N. C.)

INDIAN GAP   5266 ft.
West of Newfound Gap, along road to Clingmans Dome (Tenn.–N. C.)

JONAS CREEK   approx. 2400–4825 ft.
Tributary of Forney Creek between Welch Ridge and Forney Ridge (N. C.)

KANATI FORK   approx. 3050–4340 ft.
Tributary of Oconaluftee River, north of Thomas Divide (N. C.)

KEPHART PRONG   approx. 2800–5400 ft.
Tributary of the Oconaluftee River, above Smokemont (N. C.)

LAUREL BRANCH   approx. 2450–3900 ft.
Tributary of Middle Prong of Little Pigeon River in Greenbrier section (Tenn.)

LAUREL CREEK   approx. 1200–1800 ft.
Tributary of the Middle Prong of Little River; along spur road to Cades Cove (Tenn.)

LE CONTE LODGE   approx. 6300 ft.
Near summit of Mt. Le Conte, at junction of trails (Tenn.)

LITTLE RIVER   approx. 1100–5350 ft.
Originates north of Mt. Buckley; leaves Park at northwestern boundary near Tremont Y (Tenn.)

LITTLE RIVER ROAD   approx. 1100–2320 ft.
From Sugarlands Visitor Center to vicinity of Townsend (Tenn.)

LOW GAP   4242 ft.
On state line, north of Cosby Knob, in northeastern part of Park (Tenn.)

LOW GAP TRAIL   2500–4242 ft.
Trail from Cosby Campground to Low Gap (Tenn.)

MADDRON BALD TRAIL   3100–5500 ft.
Between Indian Camp Creek and Snake Den Mountain in Cosby section (Tenn.)

MEIGS CREEK   approx. 1400–3300 ft.
Tributary of Little River, joining Little River between The Sinks and the Tremont Y (Tenn.)

MESSER FORK   approx. 2900–4700 ft.
Tributary of Rough Fork, southwest of Cataloochee (N. C.)

METCALF BOTTOMS   1679 ft.
Picnic area along Little River, 2 miles above The Sinks bridge (Tenn.)

MIDDLE PRONG OF LITTLE PIGEON RIVER   1374–1680 ft.
Flows from Greenbrier to Emerts Cove (Tenn.)

MINGUS AND COOPER CREEK DIVIDE   approx. 3500 ft.
Ridge between Mingus and Cooper Creeks near southern boundary of Park (N. C.)

MOORES SPRING SHELTER   4700 ft.
Along Appalachian Trail east of Gregory Bald (Tenn.–N. C.)

MT. BUCKLEY   6582 ft. (summit)
One mile west of Clingmans Dome on state line (Tenn.–N. C.)

MT. CAMMERER   5025 ft. (summit)
Near state line in extreme northeast corner of Park (Tenn.)

MT. COLLINS   6188 ft. (summit)
On state line between Indian Gap and Clingmans Dome (Tenn.–N. C.)

MT. GUYOT   6621 ft. (summit)
On state line east of Greenbrier (Tenn.–N. C.)

MT. KEPHART   approx. 6200 ft. (summit)
On state line 3 miles northeast of Newfound Gap (Tenn.–N. C.)

MT. LE CONTE   6593 ft. (summit)
Third highest peak in Park; southeast of Gatlinburg (Tenn.)

MT. STERLING   5835 ft. (summit)
Near eastern boundary of Park, south of town of Mt. Sterling (N. C.)

MT. STERLING BALD   approx. 5800 ft.
Near summit of Mt. Sterling (N. C.)

MT. STERLING CREEK   approx. 3464–4900 ft.
Drains Mt. Sterling Ridge north of Mt. Sterling Gap (N. C.)

NEWFOUND GAP   5040 ft.
Highest point on transmountain road; on state line and along Appalachian Trail (Tenn.–N. C.)

NEWT PRONG   approx. 2808–4460 ft.
Tributary of Jakes Creek, above Elkmont (Tenn.)

NOISY CREEK   approx. 1550–3600 ft.
Tributary of Webb Creek, flowing between Greenbrier Pinnacle and U. S. Rt. 73 (Tenn.)

NOLAND CREEK   approx. 2600–5200 ft.
Between Forney Ridge and Noland Divide (N. C.)

NOLAND DIVIDE   2000–6000 ft.
From east of Clingmans Dome south to Deep Creek Campground (N. C.)

OCONALUFTEE RIVER   approx. 1950–3050 ft.
Flows along transmountain road to southern boundary of Park (N. C.)

OCONALUFTEE VISITOR CENTER   approx. 2100 ft.
Along transmountain road 2 miles north of Cherokee (N. C.)

OLD BLACK MOUNTAIN   6356 ft. (summit)
On state line 1 mile north of Mt. Guyot (Tenn.–N. C.)

PARK HEADQUARTERS   1460 ft.
Area 2 miles south of Gatlinburg (Tenn.)

PARK HEADQUARTERS BUILDING   1460 ft.
Administration Building, 2 miles south of Gatlinburg (Tenn.)

PARSON BALD   4730 ft.
On state line west of Gregory Bald (Tenn.–N. C.)

PARSONS BRANCH   approx. 1350–2650 ft.
Between Hannah Mountain and southwestern boundary of Park (N. C.)

PAULS GAP   approx. 4500 ft.
Vicinity of southeastern boundary of Park (N. C.)

PECKS CORNER   approx. 5600 ft.
On state line east of Charlies Bunion (Tenn.–N. C.)

PILOT RIDGE   approx. 3000 ft.
Along southern boundary of Park near Forney Creek (N. C.)

PIN OAK GAP   4428 ft.
On Balsam Mountain, north of Heintooga Overlook (N. C.)

PINE KNOT BRANCH   approx. 3000–3600 ft.
Tributary of the Little River arising near Cove Mountain (Tenn.)

PINNACLE CREEK   1791–3900 ft.
Tributary of Eagle Creek, between Thunderhead and Fontana Reservoir (N. C.)

PROCTER   1700 ft.
Abandoned town north of Fontana Lake along Hazel Creek (N. C.)

PROCTER CREEK   approx. 3060–4500 ft.
Flows from near Appalachian Trail to Hazel Creek (N. C.)

RAINBOW FALLS TRAIL   2581–6300 ft.
From Cherokee Orchard to Mt. Le Conte via Rocky Spur (Tenn.)

RAVENSFORD   2100 ft.
Near junction of Raven Fork and Oconaluftee River; in vicinity of Oconaluftee Visitor Center (N. C.)

ROARING FORK   approx. 1300 ft. (mouth)
Enters West Prong of Little Pigeon River in Gatlinburg; originates north of Cliff Top on Mt. Le Conte (Tenn.)

ROUNDBOTTOM   3022 ft.
On Straight Fork, at junction with Roundbottom Creek; southeastern part of Park (N. C.)

SALTPETER CAVE   1750 ft.
Near Park boundary, between Dry Valley and Whiteoak Sink (Tenn.)

SCHOOLHOUSE GAP   approx. 2000 ft.
On northern boundary of Park on old road between Whiteoak Sink (vicinity) and Dry Valley in Tuckaleechee Cove (Tenn.)

SHEEP PEN GAP   4610 ft.
On state line west of Gregory Bald (Tenn.–N. C.)

SHUCKSTACK TOWER   3824 ft.
Fire tower north of Fontana Lake (N. C.)

SILERS BALD   5620 ft.
On state line west of Clingmans Dome (Tenn.–N. C.)

SINKING CREEK   approx. 3750–5050 ft.
Tributary of Big Creek, east of Mt. Guyot (Tenn.)

SINKS, THE (or The Sinks bridge)   1565 ft.
Along Little River Road below Metcalf Bottoms (Tenn.)

SMOKEMONT (and Campground area)   2198 ft.
On transmountain road above Oconaluftee Visitor Center (N. C.)

SNAKE DEN MOUNTAIN   approx. 5500 ft. (summit)
West of Cosby Campground (Tenn.)

SPENCE FIELD   approx. 5000 ft.
Just west of Thunderhead on state line (Tenn.–N. C.)

SPRUCE MOUNTAIN approx. 5600 ft. (summit)
Near Heintooga Ridge (N. C.)

STRAIGHT FORK approx. 2400–4000 ft.
Tributary of Raven Fork, between Hyatt Ridge and Balsam Mt., in eastern part of Park (N. C.)

SUGARLAND MOUNTAIN 5720 ft. (summit)
Between Little River and West Prong of Little Pigeon River (Tenn.)

SUGARLANDS 1500–2700 ft.
Valley from near Sugarlands Visitor Center to Chimneys Campground (Tenn.)

TAPOCO 1100 ft.
Town just outside southwestern boundary of Park (N. C.)

THOMAS RIDGE mostly 4000–5000 ft.
Main divide west of the Oconaluftee River (N. C.)

THUNDERHEAD 5530 ft. (summit)
On state line southeast of Cades Cove (Tenn.–N. C.)

TOWNSEND 1100 ft.
Town in Tuckaleechee Cove, 2 miles north of Park boundary (Tenn.)

TRANSMOUNTAIN ROAD 1300–5040 ft.
Road from Gatlinburg, Tenn., to Cherokee, N. C., via Newfound Gap (Tenn.–N. C.)

TREMONT 1925 ft.
On Middle Prong of Little River near junction with Lynn Camp Prong (Tenn.)

TREMONT Y 1150 ft.
Junction of Little River and Middle Prong of Little River (Tenn.)

TRILLIUM GAP 4717 ft.
Between Mt. Le Conte and Brushy Mountain (Tenn.)

TROUT BRANCH approx. 3600 ft. (mouth)
Tributary of West Prong of Little Pigeon River; along transmountain road above the Loop Tunnel (Tenn.)

TWENTYMILE CREEK 1313–4150 ft.
Flows into Cheoah Lake on Park boundary west of Fontana Dam (N. C.)

WALKER CREEK approx. 3250–4675 ft.
Tributary of Hazel Creek (N. C.)

WALKER PRONG approx. 4750 ft. (mouth)
Tributary of West Prong of Little Pigeon River (Tenn.)

WALNUT BOTTOMS 3042 ft.
On Big Creek, in northeastern part of Park (N. C.)

WEARS COVE   1454 ft.
On Park boundary north of Cove Mt. (Tenn.)

WEST PRONG OF LITTLE PIGEON RIVER (same as West Fork of Little Pigeon River)   approx. 1300–4600 ft.
Main stream along road from Gatlinburg, Tenn., to near Newfound Gap (Tenn.)

WHITEOAK SINK   approx. 1750 ft.
Small cove just inside Park boundary, northeast of Cades Cove (Tenn.)

WHITE ROCK (see Mt. Cammerer)

Glossary

AESTIVATION. Inactivity during the summer

ALBINO. An animal lacking normal pigmentation; characterized by having white fur and pink eyes

ARBOREAL. Living in trees

BOREAL. Pertaining to the north

CARNIVORE. A flesh-eating mammal

CARNIVOROUS. Eating or living on flesh

CARRION. Dead or putrefying flesh; a carcass

CLIMAX. A relatively stable community of plants and animals dominant in a given locality

CONIFER. Evergreen shrub or tree characterized by needle-shaped leaves, cones, and a resinous wood; includes the pines, spruces, firs, and junipers

COPULATION. The act of uniting in sexual intercourse

DECIDUOUS. In botany, the falling off or shedding of leaves at specific seasons; not evergreen

DIURNAL. Active during the daytime

DORMANCY. A period of inactivity, usually lasting weeks or months

ECOLOGICAL SUCCESSION. The process by which one type of plant community replaces another, leading eventually to the climax community

ECOLOGY. The study of the relationship of animals to their environment

EXTIRPATION. The complete removal of a species from a locality where it once lived

EXTINCTION. The complete removal of all members of a species from the face of the earth

FALLOW. Land left unseeded after plowing

FAUNA. The animals living within a given area

FECES. Animal excrement

FERAL. Undomesticated; living in a wild state

FORAGE. To search for food

FOSSORIAL. Living in a burrow or hole in the ground

FULL-TERM EMBRYO. An embryo that is ready to be born

GESTATION. The period of development of an embryo from conception until birth

HABITAT. The specific area where a species or an individual animal usually lives

HERBACEOUS VEGETATION. Seed plants devoid of woody tissue which die completely, or down to the ground, after flowering

HIBERNACULUM. The place where an animal hibernates

HIBERNATION. Inactivity during the winter

HYBRIDIZE. To crossbreed; to produce hybrid individuals

IMPLANTATION. The process by which the developing embryo attaches to the lining of the uterus

INCISORS. Teeth in the front of the jaw adapted for cutting

INSECTIVOROUS. To feed upon insects

INVERTEBRATE. An animal without a spinal column: insects, spiders, millipedes, etc.

MARSUPIAL. A member of the order Marsupialia; the females typically lack a placenta and carry their young in a marsupium

MARSUPIUM. A pouch on the abdomen of marsupials; used for carrying young

MAST. The fruit of the oak, beech, and other trees

MELANISM. The development of dark coloring matter in the skin, hair, etc., due to extreme pigmentation; opposed to albinism

METABOLISM. The aggregate of all chemical and physical processes constantly taking place in a living organism

MIGRATE. To move periodically from one region to another

MOLT. The shedding of hair in preparation for replacement by new growth

NOCTURNAL. Active at night

OMNIVOROUS. Eating both animal and vegetable food

OVULATION. The release of an egg from the ovary of a female

PELAGE. The coat or covering of a mammal

PELT. The skin of a fur-bearing mammal

PLEISTOCENE EPOCH. The first of the two epochs of the Quaternary period of geologic time, characterized by ice sheets over much of the northern hemisphere

POLYGAMOUS. An individual that mates with several of the opposite sex

PREDATION. The process of killing another animal for food

PREDATOR. A species that kills another

PREHENSILE. Adapted for grasping or coiling around and clinging to objects

PREY. Any animal seized by another for food

PROLIFIC. To produce many offspring

RETRACTILE. Capable of being drawn back or in, as a cat's claws

SCAT. Animal excrement

SUBMAXILLARY GLAND. One of the salivary glands, situated near the angle of the lower jaw

SUBTERRANEAN. Situated or occurring below the surface of the earth

TALUS. A sloping mass of rock fragments at the base of a cliff

TOPOGRAPHY. The description of the physical features of an area

VEGETARIAN. An animal that eats only vegetable foods

Literature Cited

ADAMS, D. A. 1950. *Myotis subulatus leibii* in North Carolina. J. Mammal. 31(1):97–98.

ALCOA NEWS 1941. March 3, 1941. 12(5):2.

ALLEN, J. A. 1876. The American Bisons, living and extinct. Mem. Kentucky Geol. Survey, Vol. 1, pt. 2. 246 p.

AUDUBON, J. J., AND J. BACHMAN 1846. The viviparous quadrupeds of North America, Vol. 1. J. J. Audubon, New York. 389 p.

BARBOUR, R. W. 1951. The mammals of Big Black Mountain, Harlan County, Kentucky. J. Mammal. 32(1):100–110.

BARKALOW, F. S. 1967. Range extension and notes on the least weasel in North Carolina. J. Mammal. 48(3):488.

BLAIR, W. F., A. P. BLAIR, P. BRODKORB, F. R. CAGLE, AND G. A. MOORE. 1968. Vertebrates of the United States. McGraw-Hill, New York. 616 p.

BREWER, C. 1964. June 28, 1964. Hike recalls tales of tall guide, panther wrestling. The Knoxville News-Sentinel, Knoxville.

BRIMLEY, C. S. 1944–1946. The mammals of North Carolina. 18 installments in Carolina Tips. Carolina Biol. Supply Co., Elon College, N. C. 36 p.

BUCKLEY, S. B. 1859. Mountains of North Carolina and Tennessee. The Amer. J. Sci. and Arts, Ser. 2, 27:286–294.

BURT, W. H., AND R. P. GROSSENHEIDER 1952. A field guide to the mammals. Riverside Press, Cambridge, Mass. 200 p.

CHURCH, M. L. 1925. *Mustela allegheniensis* in North Carolina. J. Mammal. 6(4):281.

CONAWAY, C. H., AND D. W. PFITZER 1952. *Sorex palustris* and *Sorex dispar* from the Great Smoky Mountains National Park. J. Mammal. 33(1):106–108.

CONAWAY, C. H., AND J. C. HOWELL 1953. Observations on the mammals of Johnson and Carter Counties, Tennessee, and Avery County, North Carolina. J. Tenn. Acad. Sci. 28(1):53–61.

COPE, E. D. 1870. Observations on the fauna of the southern Alleghanies. Amer. Nat. 4(7):392–402.

EDWARDS, M. G. 1963. Wildlife comes to the city. Wildlife in North Carolina, pp. 8–9.

FLEETWOOD, R. J.   1934–1935.   Journal of Raymond J. Fleetwood, wildlife technician, Great Smoky Mountains National Park, for the period May 27, 1934–June 27, 1935. 499 p. (typewritten).

GANIER, A. F.   1928.   The wild life of Tennessee. J. Tenn. Acad. Sci. 3(3):10–22.

GANIER, A. F., AND A. CLEBSCH   1946.   Breeding birds of the Unicoi Mountains. Migrant 17(4):53–59.

GOLLEY, F. B.   1962.   Mammals of Georgia. Univ. of Georgia Press, Athens. 218 p.

GORDON, R. E., AND J. R. BAILEY   1963.   The occurrence of *Parascalops breweri* on the Highlands (North Carolina) Plateau. J. Mammal. 44(3):580–581.

GRIMES, S. A.   1952.   Photographing the red-breasted nuthatch. Chat 16: 80–81.

HALL, E. R., AND E. L. COCKRUM   1953.   A synopsis of the North American microtine rodents. Univ. Kansas Publ. Nat. Hist. 5:373–498.

HALL, E. R., AND K. R. KELSON   1959.   The mammals of North America. Ronald Press, New York. 1083 p.

HAMILTON, W. J., JR.   1943.   The mammals of eastern United States. Comstock Publ. Co., Ithaca, N. Y. 432 p.
1944.   The biology of the little short-tailed shrew, *Cryptotis parva*. J. Mammal. 25(1):1–7.

HAMNETT, W. L., AND D. C. THORNTON   1953.   Tar Heel wildlife. North Carolina Wildlife Resources Commission, Raleigh. 98 p.

HANDLEY, C. O., JR.   1953.   A new flying squirrel from the southern Appalachian Mountains. Proc. Biol. Soc. Wash. 66:191–194.

HAYWOOD, J.   1823.   The natural and aboriginal history of Tennessee up to the first settlements therein by the white people in the year 1768. G. Wilson, Nashville. 390 p.

HOFFMEISTER, D. F.   1968. Pigmy shrew, *Microsorex hoyi winnemana*, in Great Smoky Mountains National Park. J. Mammal. 49(2):331.

HOLSINGER, J. R.   1964.   The gray *Myotis* in Virginia. J. Mammal. 45(1):151–152.

HOOPER, E. T.   1942.   The water shrew (*Sorex palustris*) of the southern Allegheny Mountains. Occ. Papers Mus. Zool. Univ. Mich. 463:1–4.
1958.   The male phallus in mice of the genus *Peromyscus*. Misc. Publ. Mus. Zool. Univ. Mich. 105:1–24.

HOWELL, A. H.   1909.   Notes on the distribution of certain mammals in the southeastern United States. Proc. Biol. Soc. Wash. 22(9):55–68.

HOWELL, J. C., AND C. H. CONAWAY 1952. Observations on the mammals of the Cumberland Mountains of Tennessee. J. Tenn. Acad. Sci. 27(2): 153–158.

HUHEEY, J. E., AND A. STUPKA 1967. Amphibians and reptiles of Great Smoky Mountains National Park. Univ. of Tenn. Press, Knoxville. 98 p.

HUNNICUTT, S. J. 1926. 20 years hunting and fishing in the Great Smoky Mountains. S. B. Newman and Co., Knoxville. 216 p.

JACKSON, H. H. T. 1928. A taxonomic review of the American long-tailed shrews. North American Fauna No. 51. U. S. Govt. Printing Office, Washington, D. C. 238 p.

JENKINS, J. H., AND D. W. JOHNSTON 1950. Additional records of the jumping mouse, *Zapus hudsonius*, from Georgia. J. Mammal. 31(4):461.

JOHNSTON, D. W. 1967. Ecology and distribution of mammals at Highlands, North Carolina. J. Elisha Mitchell Sci. Soc. 83(2):88–98.

JONES, P. 1957. A historical study of the European wild boar in North Carolina. MS Thesis. Appalachian State Teachers College, Boone, N. C. 100 p.

KELLOGG, R. 1937. Annotated list of West Virginia mammals. Proc. U. S. Nat. Mus. 84(3022):443–479.

——— 1939. Annotated list of Tennessee mammals. Proc. U. S. Nat. Mus. 86(3051):245–303.

KEPHART, H. 1921. Our southern highlanders. Macmillan, New York. 395 p.

KOMAREK, E. V. 1932. Distribution of *Microtus chrotorrhinus*, with description of a new subspecies. J. Mammal. 13(2):155–158.

KOMAREK, E. V., AND R. KOMAREK 1938. Mammals of the Great Smoky Mountains. Bull. Chicago Acad. Sci. 5(6):137–162.

LANMAN, C. 1849. Letters from the Alleghany Mountains. Geo. P. Putnam, New York. 198 p.

LINZEY, A. V., AND D. W. LINZEY 1967. *Microtus pennsylvanicus* in North Carolina and Tennessee. J. Mammal. 48(2):310.

LINZEY, D. W. 1966. The life history, ecology and behavior of the golden mouse, *Ochrotomys n. nuttalli,* in the Great Smoky Mountains National Park. Ph.D. Thesis. Cornell Univ., Ithaca, N. Y. 176 p.

——— 1968. An ecological study of the golden mouse, *Ochrotomys nuttalli,* in the Great Smoky Mountains National Park. Amer. Midl. Nat. 79(2):320–345.

LINZEY, D. W., AND A. V. LINZEY 1966. A second record of the meadow jumping mouse in eastern Tennessee. J. Mammal. 47(1):123.

——— 1967a. Maturational and seasonal molts in the golden mouse, *Ochrotomys nuttalli.* J. Mammal. 48(2):236–241.

1967b. Growth and development of the golden mouse, *Ochrotomys nuttalli nuttalli*. J. Mammal. 48(3):445–458.

1968. Mammals of the Great Smoky Mountains National Park. J. Elisha Mitchell Sci. Soc. 84(3):384–414.

MARSTON, M. A. 1942. Winter relations of bobcats to white-tailed deer in Maine. J. Wildl. Mgmt. 6(4):328–337.

MAYNARD, C. J. 1889. Singular effects produced by the bite of a short-tailed shrew, *Blarina brevicauda*. Contrib. to Sci. 1:57.

McCARLEY, W. H. 1954. The ecological distribution of the *Peromyscus leucopus* species group in eastern Texas. Ecology 35(3):375–379.

MERRIAM, C. H. 1888. Remarks on the fauna of the Great Smoky Mountains; with description of a new species of red-backed mouse (*Evotomys Carolinensis*). Amer. J. Sci. Ser. 3, 36(216):458–460.

MILLER, F. H. 1938. Brief narrative descriptions of the vegetative types in the Great Smoky Mountains National Park. Report to the Superintendent, Great Smoky Mountains National Park. 17 p. (typewritten).

MILLER, G. S., AND G. M. ALLEN 1928. The American bats of the genera *Myotis* and *Pizonyx*. U. S. Nat. Mus. Bull. 144. Smithsonian Institution, Washington, D. C. 218 p.

MILLER, G. S., AND R. KELLOGG 1955. List of North American recent mammals. U. S. Nat. Mus. Bull. 205. Smithsonian Institution, Washington, D. C. 954 p.

ODUM, E. P. 1948a. *Synaptomys* on the Highlands, North Carolina, Plateau. J. Mammal. 29(1):74.

1948b. *Microtus* from the piedmont of Georgia. J. Mammal. 29(1):74.

1949. Small mammals of the Highlands (North Carolina) Plateau. J. Mammal. 30(2):179–192.

PALMER, R. S. 1954. The mammal guide. Doubleday and Co., Garden City, N. Y. 384 p.

PARADISO, J. L. 1959. A new star-nosed mole (*Condylura*) from the southeastern United States. Proc. Biol. Soc. Wash. 72:103–108.

PARK NEWS AND VIEWS 1955–1969. Bimonthly newsletter of Great Smoky Mountains National Park. Gatlinburg, Tenn.

PARMALEE, P. W. 1960. A prehistoric record of the fisher in Georgia. J. Mammal. 41(3):409–410.

PARMALEE, P. W., AND J. E. GUILDAY 1966. A recent record of porcupine from Tennessee. J. Tenn. Acad. Sci. 41(3):81–82.

PAUL, J. R., AND T. L. QUAY 1963. Notes on the mammalian fauna of the Toxaway River gorge, North Carolina. J. Elisha Mitchell Sci. Soc. 79(2):124–126.

PEARSON, O. P. 1942. On the cause and nature of a poisonous action produced by the bite of a shrew (*Blarina brevicauda*). J. Mammal. 23(2):159–166.

PETRIDES, G. A. 1948. The jumping mouse in Georgia. J. Mammal. 29(1):75–76.

PFITZER, D. W. 1950. Report on mammals collected or observed, June–October, 1950 (typewritten).

RAINEY, D. G. 1956. Eastern woodrat, *Neotoma floridana*: life history and ecology. Univ. Kansas Publ. Mus. Nat. Hist. 8(10):535–646.

RAMSEY, J. G. M. 1853. The annals of Tennessee to the end of the eighteenth century: comprising its settlement, as the Watauga Association, from 1769 to 1777; a part of North Carolina, from 1777 to 1784; the State of Franklin, from 1784 to 1788; a part of North Carolina, from 1788 to 1790; the Territory of the United States, south of the Ohio, from 1790 to 1796; the State of Tennessee, from 1796 to 1800. Lippincott, Grambo and Co., Philadelphia. 744 p.

RHOADS, S. N. 1896. Contributions to the zoology of Tennessee. No. 3: mammals. Proc. Phila. Acad. Nat. Sci. 48:175–205.

ROWAN, W. 1945. Numbers of young in the common black and grizzly bears in western Canada. J. Mammal. 26(2):197–199.

1947. A case of six cubs in the common black bear. J. Mammal. 28(4): 404–405.

SAVAGE, T. 1967. The diet of rattlesnakes and copperheads in the Great Smoky Mountains National Park. Copeia 1.226–227.

SCHWARTZ, A. 1954. A second record of *Myotis subulatus leibii* in North Carolina. J. Elisha Mitchell Sci. Soc. 70(2):88–96.

1955. A record of the smoky shrew, *Sorex f. fumeus* Miller, in South Carolina. J. Mammal. 36(2):286–287.

1956. A new subspecies of the longtail shrew (*Sorex dispar* Batchelder) from the southern Appalachian mountains. J. Elisha Mitchell Sci. Soc. 72(1): 24–30.

SHANKS, R. E. 1954. Climates of the Great Smoky Mountains. Ecology 35:354–361.

SMITH, E. R., J. B. FUNDERBURG, JR., AND T. L. QUAY 1960. A checklist of North Carolina mammals. N. C. Wildl. Resources Comm., Raleigh. 19 p.

STEGEMAN, L. C. 1938. The European wild boar in the Cherokee National Forest, Tennessee. J. Mammal. 19(3):279–290.

STUPKA, A. 1935–1962. Nature journal, Great Smoky Mountains National Park. 28 vols. (years) each with index (typewritten).

1938a. Report to the 32nd convention of the International Association of Game and Fish and Conservation Commissioners. Asheville, N. C. 119 p.

1960a. Second specimen of least weasel from North Carolina. J. Mammal. 41(4):519–520.

1960b. Great Smoky Mountains National Park. Natural History Handbook Series No. 5. Govt. Printing Office, Washington, D. C. 75 p.

1963. Notes on the birds of Great Smoky Mountains National Park. Univ. of Tenn. Press, Knoxville. 242 p.

1964. Trees, shrubs, and woody vines of Great Smoky Mountains National Park. Univ. of Tenn. Press, Knoxville. 186 p.

TAYLOR, W. P. 1956. The deer of North America. The Stackpole Co., Harrisburg, Pa. 668 p.

TUTTLE, M. D. 1964a. Additional record of *Sorex longirostris* in Tennessee. J. Mammal. 45(1):146–147.

1964b. *Myotis subulatus* in Tennessee. J. Mammal. 45(1):148–149.

1968. First Tennessee record of *Mustela nivalis*. J. Mammal. 49(1):133.

WHITTAKER, R. H. 1956. Vegetation of the Great Smoky Mountains. Ecol. Monographs 26:1–80.

WIMSATT, W. A. 1942. Survival of spermatozoa in the female reproductive tract of the bat. Anat. Rec. 83(2):299–307.

1944. Further studies on the survival of spermatozoa in the female reproductive tract of the bat. Anat. Rec. 88(2):193–204.

WOODS, F. W., AND R. E. SHANKS 1957. Replacement of chestnut in the Great Smoky Mountains of Tennessee and North Carolina. J. Forestry 55(11):847.

YOUNG, S. P. 1958. The Bobcat of North America. The Stackpole Co., Harrisburg, Pa. 193 p.

YOUNG, S. P., AND H. H. T. JACKSON 1951. The clever Coyote. The Stackpole Co., Harrisburg, Pa. 411 p.

Index